RESISTING DENIAL,
REFUSING DESPAIR

RESISTING DENIAL, REFUSING DESPAIR

—And Other Essays—

Walter Brueggemann

CASCADE *Books* · Eugene, Oregon

RESISTING DENIAL, REFUSING DESPAIR
And Other Essays

Cascade Books
An Imprint of Wipf and Stock Publishers
199 W. 8th Ave., Suite 3
Eugene, OR 97401

www.wipfandstock.com

PAPERBACK ISBN: 978-1-6667-1514-9
HARDCOVER ISBN: 978-1-6667-1515-6
EBOOK ISBN: 978-1-6667-1516-3

Cataloging-in-Publication data:

Names: Brueggemann, Walter, author.

Title: Resisting denial, refusing despair : and other essays / Walter Brueggemann.

Description: Eugene, OR: Cascade Books, 2021. | Includes bibliographical references and indexes.

Identifiers: ISBN: 978-1-6667-1514-9 (PAPERBACK). | ISBN: 978-1-6667-1515-6 (HARDCOVER). | ISBN: 978-1-6667-1516-3 (EBOOK).

Subjects: LCSH: Bible. OT—Criticism, interpretation, etc. | Church and social problems. | United States—Religion—21st century.

Classification: BS1192.5 B825 2022 (print). | BS1192.5 (epub).

VERSION NUMBER 082922

CONTENTS

PREFACE

I AM GLAD TO make available these several pieces of the critical imagination allowed me in my old age. The only continuing resolve I have in these pieces is to try to live honestly at the interface between the testimony of Scripture and our life in the world as God's well-loved creatures. It is evident for me, as for any who undertake such work, that this interface is inexhaustibly generative, both in terms of God's assurances and in the summons of the God of the Gospel to live differently in the world.

I have had no general thematic (beyond that interface), as I have moved from piece to piece, from topic to topic. Nevertheless two themes do recur in these pieces. First, that we are destined by the gospel to live *in the public world of politics and economics.* Enlightenment rationality has been quite content, even eager, to let "religion" have a free rein in personal, familial, and domestic matters, as long as it did not intrude into the public spheres of money and power. To some great extent the church in our culture has been content to collude in this domestication of faith. But of course the Bible insists otherwise, as all of the covenantal, prophetic, and sapiential traditions of the Old Testament together attest that the practice of faith pertains to all the spheres of life where the well-being of the neighbor is at stake. And, of course, it is not different in the New Testament, as the gospel anticipates a "kingdom" that is sharply alternative to the kingdoms of this age. I have tried in these pieces to bear witness to the force of faith in the face of the force of empire. My several pieces on the narrative of Naboth's vineyard attest that the rule of God pertains to such public realties.

Second, these pieces variously reflect my conviction that faith calls us to be *critically and differently engaged* in the life of the world. "Critically and differently" means that we attend, as best we can, to the will and purpose of God for our lives in the neighborhood. Attentiveness to that will and purpose means that we live by different norms, rely on different assurances, and answer to different summons. Thus my lead piece on "resistance and refusal" is thematic for the stance of the faithful church, even while the actual institutional church has been less resistant and less refusing than we have intended.

It is my hope that this collection may be useful for the teaching, preaching work of the church as we do the serious obedience of *being differently and critically engaged in our public life.* The matter is urgent, given the immense gap between the "haves" and "have-nots" in our economy, and given the deep jeopardy in which our democracy now stands.

I am glad to acknowledge the great support of my "usual suspects." I am grateful to Mary Brown, who first accepted these pieces for her blog platform, *church.anew*. And I am yet again grateful to K. C. Hanson for his acceptance of these pieces for publication, and for his energetic editorial work which he has done to complete the manuscript. I am abidingly grateful to Tia Brueggemann, who has carefully proofed and edited each of my efforts to make them legible and coherent.

It will be evident that much of my work is triggered by my continuing to read fresh publications. For that reason I also express great thanks to the Traverse City District Library and its staff for its willing capacity to meet my reading needs and hopes. I take regular liberty, in these pieces, to cite my new reading, not only because such reading is crucial for me, but because I have more time to read than many other readers, and I hope my citations may prove useful in guiding the reading of others. My choices of titles for reading are inescapably subjective, but I am glad to share them.

I am even more glad to imagine the readership of this manuscript as a company of those who are engaged in the practice of serious faith in the world where God's rule is most often hidden from us. I am glad, as I am able, to be in solidarity with those who continue to insist that the rule of the God of faithful justice matters to the life of our society. Thus I finish with great gratitude to my readers, to Mary Brown, to K. C. Hanson, to Tia Brueggemann, to the District Library, and to the company of those who receive my work as I have intended it.

Walter Brueggemann
Columbia Theological Seminary

1

RESISTING DENIAL,
REFUSING DESPAIR

THE CHURCH IS NOW driven back to basics! We are driven there
in the context of the dominant narrative of our society that is a
narrative of *scarcity, fear, greed, and violence*. That narrative is all
around us and is powerfully compelling among us and for almost
all of us. It is clear that the outcome of that narrative is likely to be
denial for which former President Trump is a lead player. This is a
narrative of denial, not wanting to see reality for what it is. I suggest that the former president knows, as most of us know, that the
reason for denial is that when we see the reality of our current life,
we will plunge into *despair*. Thus, *denial* serves to protect us from
despair. I suggest that if we live by that narrative we are surely fated
to *either denial or despair*. When we see the reality of our life (the
virus, the economic meltdown, the crisis of climate, the jeopardy
of democratic institutions), we are pressed toward helplessness
because the issues appear to be too immense for effective address.

In that context as we ponder the basics of our faith we are
promptly aware that we in the community of the baptized inhabit
a very different narrative that contradicts that dominant narrative.
The narrative of our faith has many variant forms of articulation.

At its center, in any case, is the *Friday–Sunday drama* of *execution and resurrection.* It is my thought that as a new season begins in the life of the church this drama of execution–resurrection might govern our reason and our imagination in surprising and generative ways.

This Friday moment of our faith, signified by darkness, is a moment of profound loss that evokes deep grief. The church is always tempted to compromise that profound loss (like leaving the last light on at Tenebrae). But the loss is total; the Messiah did die! We have reached the null point of reality. The disciples were driven to bewilderment and despair by Friday night: "We had hoped . . ." (Luke 24:21). It is a moment of loss, grief, and honesty that contradicts the seduction of denial by its truth-telling insistence. Thus, the church, with this basic narrative, does not flinch from the loss all around us. It tells the truth about the loss of the old world in a way that permits relinquishment of what is gone. Think what is gone! The naming of what is gone assures that the church will not be the "happiest place in town." It is not, however, the work of the church to be happy, but to be honest; honesty, then and now, requires grief for loss.

Friday in our drama of faith is countered (countered, not simply followed!) by Sunday, by the inscrutable gift of new Easter life in a world that had been shut down in despair. If Saturday invites despair, Easter is the great counter to despair that invites to hope. This is hope in the power of God to give life in the midst of death: This is the God "who gives life to the dead and calls into existence the things that do not exist" (Rom 4:17).

> Our hope is in no other save in thee;
> our faith is built upon thy promise free;
> Lord, give us peace, and make us calm and sure,
> that in thy strength we ever more endure.[1]

It is the work of the church to engage in hope that is neither optimism nor a notion of progress, but a confession that God's resolve

---

1. John Calvin, "I Greet Thee Who My Sure Redeemer Art," in *Glory to God*, 624.

for a new heaven and a new earth is not precluded or hindered by the power of death, not the death of old white, male, straight privilege, not the death of US domination, not the death of any of our treasured totems:

> Our little systems have their day;
> they have their day and cease to be;
> they are but broken lights of thee;
> and Thou, O Lord, art more than they.[2]

Easter is the occasion for us to assert of God that God is "more than they," more than our treasured systems, more than our past certitudes and our privilege, deeply, wholly "more than they"!

We now live amid immense loss. Our pervasive system of white male domination and all that follows from that is being lost. While some will surely rejoice at that, many in the church feel that loss acutely. The loss, however, is a run-up to God's newness that is beyond our capacity. For that reason the church meets to recite the promises of God. God's promises, counter to our feeble capacity for newness, surprise us with newness we do not conjure or evoke, because this is the God who is able to accomplish abundantly far more than all we can ask or imagine (Eph 3:20).

The church has two principle tasks in our time, I propose:

— to practice *grief* in the face of *denial* by *truth-telling*;[3]

— to practice *hope* in the face of *despair* by *promise-telling*.

Both of these practices that are respectively grounded in *the crucifixion* and *the resurrection* counter the dominant narrative of scarcity, fear, greed, and violence. They counter frontally by the performance of abundance, courage, generosity, and peaceableness:

abundance in the face of scarcity;

courage in the face of fear;

generosity in the face of greed; and

peaceableness in the face of violence.

---

2. Tennyson, "In Memoriam A.H.H." (1833), reprinted in Turner, *Tennyson*.

3. See Brueggemann, "Truth-Telling as Subversive Obedience."

This is an urgent time to help church folk see clearly the contradiction between our narrative of faith and the narrative that dominates our society. We are a community that, for good reason,

— resists denial and tells the truth,

— refuses despair and tells the hope.

The interpreter may find rich grist for this work in the Old Testament. In the memory of Israel:

— The moment of loss is the displacement of exile. Hananiah, judged to be "false," is the voice of denial, incapable of recognizing the exile to be serious (Jer 28:2, 11). He is countered by the truth-telling of Jeremiah (v. 14)!

— The moment of hope is the time of restoration and homecoming. Despair is palpable in the community of the displaced: "Our bones are dried up, and our hope is lost; we are cut off completely" (Ezek 37:11). That despair is countered by the hope-telling of Ezekiel (vv. 12–14)!

Israel knows about both crucifixion and resurrection.[4] Israel knows about denial and despair; it resists denial and it refuses despair. Its resistance and refusal are made possible by telling a different story and performing a different practice. It is a resistance and a refusal that are performed and practiced in actual liturgical insistence.[5] Thus honest grief and buoyant hope (as alternative to denial and despair) come to full voice in Israel's *laments* and *doxologies.*

It is crucial that the counternarrative of Friday honesty about loss and Sunday joy at possibility not only be "thought" and "believed," but that it be *performed in actual, bodily, concrete ways.* There are many ways to do that performance, but at the center of such performance of the counternarrative of faith is liturgical

---

4. See Levenson, *Death and Resurrection of the Beloved Son*; Levenson, *Resurrection and the Restoration of Israel*; and Madigan and Levenson, *Resurrection.* See also Brueggemann, "Proclamation of the Resurrection."

5. On this, see Fishbane, *Sacred Attunement.*

practice. At the center of that liturgical practice, moreover, is the book of Psalms that can readily be divided into the psalms of *lament, protest, and complaint* and the psalms of *praise, thanks, and hope.*

The psalms of lament, protest, and complaint are indeed *Friday Psalms* wherein Israel—and eventually all of the faithful—voice their honest loss to God. These psalms are indeed laments as they describe in tones of discouragement and abandonment many situations in which the blessings of life are experienced as remote or absent. They are not, however, voices of resignation precisely because in addition to complaint that spells out the loss, they are psalms of protest in which the speaker insists that the present circumstance is unacceptable. The speaker hopes for, asks for, and fully expects a response from God that will effectively alter present reality.

At the center of these Friday articulations are vigorous demanding imperatives in which the speaker boldly insists to God that the speaker has legitimate expectations to which God must respond. We can find these imperatives everywhere in these poems:

> Rise up, O LORD!
>> Deliver me, O my God! (Ps 3:7)

> Answer me when I call, O God of my right! . . .
>> Be gracious to me and hear my prayer. (Ps 4:1)

> Be gracious to me, O LORD, for I am languishing
>> O LORD, heal me, for my bones are shaking with terror. (Ps 6:2)

> Give ear to my prayer, O God;
>> do not hide yourself from my supplication.
> Attend to me, and answer me. (Ps 55:1–2a)

Such vigorous imperatives on the lips of the faithful are of course unfamiliar to most Christian worshipers because our worship tends to be excessively reverential and deferential. There is no such deference here. Indeed we can notice that there is a provisional role reversal in these psalms whereby the speaker takes on the role of the pacesetter for the exchange. These psalms do not hesitate to speak out loud an insistence that God create new social possibility. We may notice, for example, in Psalm 86 that the speaker prays back to God God's own claim of fidelity and insists that God must measure up to that claim:

> But You, O Lord, are a God merciful and gracious,
>> slow to anger and abounding in steadfast love and faithfulness.
> Turn to me, and be gracious to me;
>> give strength to your servant;
>> save the child of your serving girl.
> Show me a sign of your favor.
> (Ps 86:15–17a; see Exod 34:6–7)

The psalms of *praise, thanks, and hope,* conversely, are *Sunday Psalms* that celebrate the new life that God gives. At the center of this trust in the restorative power of God is the deep rootage of the covenant tradition. Israel—and we who follow—count on and trust in God's sovereign fidelity that persists in every circumstance:

> The LORD is merciful and gracious,
>> slow to anger and abounding in steadfast love.
> He will not always accuse,
>> nor will he keep his anger forever.
> He does not deal with us according to our sins,
>> nor repay us according to our iniquities.
> (Ps 103:8–9; see Exod 34:6–7)

Israel does not doubt the capacity of God to move life beyond present unbearable circumstance; for that reason it praises and commends God in remembrance and in anticipation. In these psalms there is no longer any assertion of "me" or "my"; now the accent is turned away from the speaker to the wonder and transformative reality of God: "you," "Thou." This is the one who is the agent of active verbs of restoration, healing, and newness. In these psalms there is trust in and yielding to the wonder and goodness of God. The extreme expression of this yielding to God is the final psalm 150:

Praise the LORD!
Praise God in his sanctuary;
    praise him in his mighty firmament!
Praise him for his mighty deeds;
    praise him according to his surpassing greatness.
Praise him with trumpet sound;
    praise him with lute and harp!
Praise him with tambourine and dance;
    praise him with strings and pipe!
Praise him with clanging cymbals!
    Praise him with loud clashing cymbals!
Let everything that breaths praise the LORD!
Praise the LORD!

One can imagine the singing, dancing, and gladness as the community of faith in God moves beyond self and dire circumstance so that it may be lost in "wonder, love, and praise." In this act of glad self-abandonment, the community eschews despair; it refuses to give in to present circumstance and does not doubt the capacity and readiness of God for otherwise. This is indeed a stubborn insistent refusal of despair.

The *Friday Psalms* of lament, protest, and complaint *resist denial*. The *Sunday Psalms* of thanks and hope for new life *refuse despair*. If a Christian congregation is to engage in glad risky missional work, then it must be unfrozen from our habitual denial and despair that are the currency of our dominant narrative. The psalms are a vehicle for such an indispensable thaw. (When we fully appreciate such performance with the psalms, then we may notice that there are many other songs and poems that echo and reiterate the claims of the Psalter.)

A practical caveat: It is unmistakable that the Friday part of this dialectic is the hard part for most pastors and for most congregations. We most want to rush to the Sunday part. This is evident in the practical refusal to engage the Friday Psalms as in their absence in the sequence of the lectionary. This is evident, moreover, in the way in which most congregations slip past Good Friday with as little notice as possible in an eagerness for the exuberance of Easter. But the Sunday part without the Friday part ends in triumphalism and illusion. It is a resurrection before which there has been no crucifixion. There can be no resurrection if there is no crucifixion. There is no genuine praise if there has been no honest lament, protest, and complaint. The church and its pastors have resources for a faithful engagement with the time, place, and circumstance where God has placed us. But it will require intentional resolve to allow Friday its due in the process. There is little point, in my judgment, in the church simply echoing the pious clichés of the dominant narrative of our society. Our work—and our wonder—is to do otherwise. It is my urging that pastors and congregations may undertake this unfamiliar work that boldly *resists denial* and with equal boldness *refuses despair*.

2

PERFECT FEAR CASTS OUT LOVE

THE CHURCH IS IN the "Love Business." That is what we do. We dare make the claim that "God is love" (1 John 4:16). Our comeback to that wondrous passion of God for the world is to love back . . . love God . . . love neighbor. Indeed the way we love God is to love neighbor. When we receive the love of God and act it out toward God and neighbor, we are not afraid. We are not afraid because

> Perfect love casts out fear! (1 John 4:18)

That is the strategy we use with our young children. Our love for them overrides their fears. We may pause over this stunning statement. When we are secure in a long, reliable faithfulness, fear has no power over us; we are free to live grace-filled, unencumbered lives without looking over our shoulder. As we face this immediate brutality in our midst, it seems that the gospel proposition in the epistle is completely reversed:

> Perfect fear casts out love.

What a mouthful! "Perfect fear!" Fear that is totalizing, all-encompassing, redefining everything! Our society is now occupied by perfect fear:

— The virus lands us in fear.

— The disabled economy leaves us in fear.

— Elementally we may be fearful that the old familiar that is precious to us is evaporating before our very eyes. The old certitudes don't count for much.

— Fear-mongering has become a political strategy, because frightened people are easier to manipulate.

— And, of course, there is always the old fear of the other that can be revved up, fear of everyone who is unlike us, most obviously fear of people of color.

Fear makes love impossible. Love moves us toward the other; fear draws us away from the other. Fear turns to anger under threat. Fear turns to hate; fear easily morphs to violence. Anger, hate, violence are forms of fear that we imagine will make us safe.

The community that is in the love business might well pause over fear, name it, pay attention to it, notice it, and dissect it. We might do well to have prayers and litanies that name, in dramatic ways, the fears that summon us and notice their power for us. It is our work in love to outflank fear by greater evidence of love, by outrageous gestures and policies of love, by foolish giveaways of life's resources with nothing held back. Love is "the great giveaway" that can be acted out in terms of health, education, and housing.

We are in a contest between love and fear. It is counterintuitive for us to bet on love, but that is the bet we have made in baptism. The epistle ends with an admonition:

> Keep yourselves from idols. (1 John 5:21)

Idols are false forms of assurance. To trust such false forms of assurance is to live in fear because we know the idols cannot keep their promises to us. Every day we are in process of deciding whether love or fear is the order of the day. Now is the time for love to make a stand against fear. We make that stand by implementing our baptism in neighborly ways. Fear cannot win against love that is bold and wise for the neighborhood.

3

PERMISSION TO NARRATE

I HAVE RECENTLY SEEN this phrase "Permission to Narrate" in two interesting contexts. First, so far as I know, the phrase was coined in 1984 by Edward Said. Said was a respected academic at Columbia University. More important, he was the most outspoken advocate for Palestinian rights in Western discourse as he readily embraced his own Palestinian identity. He wrote his essay "Permission to Narrate" in the *London Review of Books* in 1984 in the wake of the war of Israel against Lebanon.[1] His commentary concerns the way in which that war was reported and championed in the West with unrestrained embrace of the Israeli cause. The phrase is Said's courageous reference to the fact that Israel and its defenders were given the "right to narrate" the war from Israel's perspective and according to Israel's interest. The Palestinians, by contrast, were denied such a right, had no advocates, and were not permitted to narrate their version of the crisis.

Said's observation of the one-sided reportage on the war concerned the way in which counter opinion had been silenced, censored, and screened out. He noted, for example, that John Chancellor on NBC had said that Israel in the war had been

1. Said, "Permission to Narrate."

"savage," but days later he retracted that statement as a "mistake." Because there was no allowance for a counternarrative, Israel's version went unchallenged in a way that was able to present the Palestinians as "terrorists."

The second usage of the phrase I have noted is by Martin Weegmann in his book titled *Permission to Narrate*.[2] The subtitle of Weegmann's book is *Explorations in Group Analysis, Psychoanalysis, Culture*. It is well known, of course, that "talk therapy," in its many variations, constitutes an opportunity for silenced selves (or that part of self that has been silenced) to be brought to speech. The accepting environment of talk therapy is a way to grant permission to narrate one's life, after that life (or that part of the self) has been silenced. Attention should also be paid to Roy Schafer, *Retelling a Life: Narrative and Dialogue in Psychoanalysis*, who, long before Weegmann, saw talk therapy as narration of the self:

> I propose that that person be viewed as a narrator, that is, as someone who, among other noteworthy actions, narrates selves. One person narrates numerous selves both in order to develop desirable (not necessarily "happy" but at least defensibly secure) versions of his or her actions and the actions of others and to act in ways that conform to those selves. In this account, there is no self that does anything. Instead there is one person telling stories about single selves, multiple selves, fragments of selves, and selves of different sorts, including *deceiving* and *deceived selves*. The narrator may, of course, attribute selves or self-states to those others, too, and others may (and do) reciprocate.[3]

These usages of the phrase set me to thinking about "permission to narrate" in the Bible, of which I will cite two witnesses. First, the elemental testimony of Israel to its exodus emancipation is in the form of a stylized narrative from parent to child:

> When you come to the land that the LORD will give you, as he has promised, you shall keep this observance [of

2. Weegmann, *Permission to Narrate*.
3. Schafer, *Retelling a Life*, 51.

Passover]. And when your children ask you, "What do you mean by this observation?" you shall say, "It is the passover sacrifice to the LORD, for he passed over the houses of the Israelites in Egypt, when he struck down the Egyptians but spared our houses." (Exod 12:25–27; see 13:8)

While this exchange is familiar to us, it is nevertheless astonishing. It is an utterance on the lips of an erstwhile slave who is willing and able to tell the children the story of enslavement and emancipation, a narrative that traffics in remembered pain and surprising freedom. This is a narrative that is grounded in a memory of suffering. It is, moreover, a narrative that would never have been "permitted" by Pharaoh as long as enslavement endured. Thus the narrating parent, in liturgical context, claims permission to narrate, to tell a story that is contrary to the dominant story of Pharaoh. In sum, Israel's entire doxological tradition pivots on this narrative of slavery and emancipation, and Israel eagerly claims permission to retell it often and vigorously.

Second, I consider the case of Bartimaeus, a blind beggar in the gospel narrative (Mark 10:46–52). Because he was a blind beggar we may conclude that he had likely been reduced to silence as an awkward embarrassment to society. But then, in the person of Jesus, he speaks! He shouts out! He breaks the long imposed silence. It is as though the presence of Jesus had given him permission so long denied to him. His utterance is brief: "Jesus, Son of David, have mercy on me" (v. 47). That is all. That, however, is an amazing narrative. It is an assertion that Bartimaeus is hoping for mercy. It is an admission that he had long been denied mercy. It is an affirmation that he trusted Jesus to be a source and giver of mercy for him. That is, this brief utterance is a bold articulation of the whole truth of Bartimaeus's life.

It is remarkable that this self-narration in this moment is met with silencing hostility. Mark says, "Many sternly ordered him to be quiet" (10:48). Luke says it was "those who were in front" (Luke 18:39). Matthew reports that it was "the crowd" that sought to silence him (20:31). This convergence of these forces suggests that many conspired (as they do!) to silence an unwelcome voice that assumes permission. All of these voices conspired together to deny permission to Bartimaeus. He, however, accepted the permission that the presence of Jesus offered him: "but he cried out even more loudly" (Mark 10:48). He would not be denied permission! By the end of the account Bartimaeus has signed on with Jesus:

> He regained his sight and followed him on the way. (10:52)

It is possible to conclude, I judge, that the rescues of Israel by YHWH (see the summary of Psalm 136) and the rescues of Jesus (see the summary of Luke 7:22) are a series of moments in which "permission to narrate" is granted that results in testimony to transformative experience. Derivatively this is what causes the church at its best to be a venue for testimonies, for narratives about the gift of new life that was not imaginable in the old contexts of domination. It follows that the church and its pastors are and must be storytellers. The church as storyteller is not for entertainment or for "sermon illustrations" or for "narrative preaching" that has become so popular. It is rather that the church should be a permission-granting community so that those who have been silenced and denied their narrative have a secure place in which their narrative can be told, received, honored, and taken seriously.

The church does not just tell stories. It is a permission-granting agency so that we do well to keep in clear purview the roster of those who are elementally denied permission to narrate their lives. In broad sweep,

— Males have permission and females do not.

— Whites have permission and people of color do not.

— Straight people have permission and gays and lesbians do not.

— Wealthy, well-educated people have permission, and poor or less-educated people do not.

— As Said has seen, Israelis have permission, and Palestinians do not.

And so on with dominating, colonizing power and the violation of those dominated and colonized.

The church has gladly known itself to be a storytelling operation. Thus we have two familiar hymns to the point:

> I love to tell the story of unseen things above,
> Of Jesus and his glory, of Jesus and his love.
> I love to tell the story, because I know 'tis true;
> It satisfies my longing as nothing else can do.[4]

> We've a story to tell to the nations,
> That shall turn their hearts to the right,
> A story of truth and mercy,
> A story of peace and light.[5]

The story the church loves to tell (and that it claims permission to tell) is the story of Jesus, "a story of peace and light" that drives darkness to dawn. Close inspection, however, shows that the version of that story told by the church is often bowdlerized and "cleaned up" to make it nice, sweet, and palatable, when in fact the story of Jesus is powerfully subversive so that it does not easily cohere with dominant interests. It strikes one that "permission to narrate" the story of crucifixion and resurrection draws to it those stories "from below," from executions at the hands of the state or of dominant culture, and from resurrections that defy imperial logic. These are stories not unlike those of the exodus that stunned Pharaoh and of Bartimaeus that repelled the crowd standing "in front." Thus, as Said has seen, the Palestinian story is unwelcome in the West. And anyone who has been engaged is serious talk therapy knows that what must be told and must be heard is most often not a pleasant or agreeable story, or one would not need special permission to narrate. And surely in the case of Jesus, what finally

4. Katherine Hankey and William G. Fischer, "I Love to Tell the Story," in *The United Methodist Hymnal*, 156.

5. H. Ernest Nichol, "We've a Story to Tell to the Nations," in *The United Methodist Hymnal*, 569.

got him executed by the state was his capacity and readiness to give permission to the narratives of those declared nonexistent by the state. That is the narrative (along with those small narratives from below that are drawn to it) that the church is entrusted to tell. This is the story we love to tell. That is the story we have to tell to the nations, all "from below" where the cry for mercy is the thematic of every utterance. The narrative for which the church has permission is precisely the story that dominant culture wants to shush.

This way of thinking has caused me to see that the church as a community has permission to narrate the true story of the world, a truth we may recognize because we see through the prism of the one crucified and risen. This suggests, moreover, that the preachers of the church have permission to go to the depth of social economic reality where mercy is absent and required, even though every preacher knows when looking out on a congregation that she has not received permission that is variously denied by the assemblage. Thus, I judge that the church and its preachers have more permission to narrate than we are most often prepared to claim.

I conclude with two reflections on the proper time for our work of narration. The wise "preacher" (Ecclesiastes) observes, as we know well:

> There is a time to keep silence,
>   and a time to speak. (Eccl 3:7b)

The trick is to know when it is the right time to speak, when it is time to narrate, when it is time to exercise permission to narrate. I suggest that many wise preachers judge many, many times when it is a proper time for silence when it may be a time to narrate the truth of the world. The word of Ecclesiastes is seconded by an odd verdict in the prophet Amos:

> Therefore the prudent will keep silent in such a time;
>   for it is an evil time. (Amos 5:13)

The term translated "prudent" might better be read as "successful" or "prosperous." Thus the verse would seem to agree with the wisdom of Eccl 3:7b; those who seek success will clam up in wisdom. In context, however, the verse in Amos may be ironic. It may be the judgment of Amos that this is no time for silence, no time for success, no time to worry about success and prospering. That surely is the burden of the rest of the book of Amos. Amos had indeed been given permission to narrate, and he does so with singular passion (see 3:3–8)! He does so, even when the high priest, Amaziah, seeks to deny him permission (Amos 7:10–17).

If we read Amos back to Said and the Palestinians and back to Weegmann and talk therapy, then it is obvious that silence and prudence cannot be the order of the day. Rather, permission to narrate requires the willful *violation of prudence* and the *transgression of silence*.

My judgment is that this is such a time in the church. We do indeed have a story to tell and we love to tell it. But the story we have to tell the nations is from below. It is a story occupied by slaves and erstwhile slaves and by such as Bartimaeus. It is a story of the urgency of mercy that every time overrides the force of silencing culture. The truth for which the church has permission to narrate is subversive. Its telling, however, is likely the only ground for hope for our society amid its deep denial and its equally deep despair.

4

BETWEEN PROMETHEAN
AND COVENANTAL TIMES

MOST OF US ARE unthinkingly committed to a certain understanding of time that we might call "Promethean." That is, we have come to regard time as something to fill, master, control, and plan out with an aim of achievement, accomplishment, success, and perhaps money-making (that is not the same as "making a living.") When we live in "Promethean time," it turns out that "sheltering" under house arrest is enormously frustrating. No doubt part of the urgency to "reopen" our public life is an urge to return to the demands and possibilities of Promethean time.

In shelter we find ourselves frustrated,

— because there is not much to *accomplish* within the limited sphere of our household;

— because there is not much to *achieve* in an environment that is non-competitive (except for an occasional board game!);

— because there is not much to *possess* when we already have within our reach everything with no more territory to conquer.

The restraints imposed upon us by sheltering resist most of our Promethean agenda; we become restless, that is, unable to enter into restorative rest.

The psalm bears witness to another way of time that we might call covenantal time:

> My times are in your hand. (Ps 31:15)

At the center of covenantal time is Sabbath rest toward which our entire week moves. We are noticing Sabbath rest all around us:

— the atmosphere is getting Sabbath from all of our pollution;

— our roads are getting Sabbath from the enormous number of accidents that have become routine;

— our children are getting Sabbath from the many illnesses that are passed around at school.

Covenantal time is marked by:

— *freedom* from burden and the insatiable need to perform and produce, so that we can center on being and not doing;

— *confident peaceableness* unlike the continual pressure of Promethean time . . . whether we have done enough or produced enough or possessed enough yet. For good reason Jesus posed the question:

> Which of you, by your anxiety,
> can add to your life even a millisecond?
> (see Matt 6:27)

— *a capacity for othering*, whereby we may attend to the other and even the vulnerable other, because I do not need to be preoccupied with myself, my gains, and my performance;

— *fidelity*, so that the next line in the psalm sounds Israel's best word for fidelity:

> Let your face shine upon your servant;
> save me in your *steadfast love*. (Ps 31:16)

It requires little imagination to see that these markings of *covenantal time*—freedom, confident peaceableness, capacity for othering, and fidelity—have no place in *Promethean time*.

It is the task and glory of the church to inhabit and to bear witness to *covenantal time* that frontally contradicts the *Promethean time* by which most of us reckon our days. The church does that by slow-time liturgy (even if online for now), by serious engagement with the vulnerable, by the wonder of baptism whereby we are named persons and not "data," and by the great festival of abundance in the Eucharist that contradicts the passionate scarcity of Promethean time, as in "I don't have enough time!"

The psalm boldly anticipates the affirmation of the *Heidelberg Catechism*, that we belong "not to ourselves, but to our faithful savior Jesus Christ." It does so of course in the confident language of Israel in the well-known prayer of 31:5:

> Into your hand I commit my spirit.

(This is the same reliable hand of God acknowledged in v. 15). On the lips of Jesus this turned out to be an appropriate prayer when he was about to be executed as an enemy of the state (Luke 23:46). Jesus was able to utter this prayer because he knew and trusted the second half of the verse of the psalm:

> You have redeemed me, O Lord, faithful God.

Indeed, this is a good prayer for our lips at the hour of our death as well. We can gladly entrust ourselves to the goodness of God in the awareness that we are indeed penultimate to the gracious self of God. But beyond the lips of Jesus at his death or our lips at our death, this prayer from the psalm is surely a good prayer every day in which we commend ourselves over to God. This prayer is a ready decision to live in covenantal time and a readiness to resist the demands of Promethean time. The trick will be to continue attention to covenantal time when we are no longer in shelter. At our best, you may watch us as we slow our motors down to a pace of gratitude.

5

RED MEAT FOR WHITE IDOLS

PAUL IS AT HIS pastoral best in his advice to the church in Corinth concerning meat for idols (1 Cor 8:1–13). He is not at all concerned with the ontological power of idols because "no idol in the world really exists" (v. 1). To the contrary, "there is but one God." For that reason he is not an absolutist and need not be. His concern rather is practical and pastoral, for he sees that devotion to idols is a divisive practice in the life of the congregation. In his practical reasoning he judges that "the strong" (those who are not at all drawn to or fearful of idols) should act in thoughtful deference for the "weak," who are more vulnerable to the illusions of the idols. His concern is that members should act in generous, gracious ways to uphold the unity and peaceableness of the faith community.

The case is not different in the Old Testament concerning idols. On the one hand, Israel knows full well that idols are "zeros" without energy, power, or authority:

> Their idols are silver and gold,
>   the work of human hands.
> They have mouths, but do not speak;
>   eyes, but do not see.
> They have ears, but do not hear;
>   noses, but do not smell.

They have hands, but do not feel;
    feet, but do not walk;
    they make no sound in their throats. (Ps 115:4–7)

They are impotent and helpless and can do nothing . . . no need to be afraid of them or to worship them. Then the psalmist adds an ominous derivative:

Those who make them are like them;
    so are all who trust in them. (v. 8)

Those who focus on what has no agency to act in the world will soon lose their agency to act in the world. It is the same in Psalm 135:

The idols of the nations are silver and gold,
    the work of human hands.
They have mouths, but do not speak;
    they have eyes but do not see;
they have ears, but they do not hear,
    and there is no breath in their mouths.
Those who make them
    and all who trust them
    shall become like them. (Ps 135:15–18)

In Isa 44:9–20 the prophet mocks the process of making idols and then trusting them. Jeremiah, moreover, dismisses the idols as an empty irrelevance:

People deck it with silver and gold;
    they fasten it with hammer and nails
    so that it cannot move.
Their idols are like scarecrows in a cucumber field,
    and they cannot speak;
they have to be carried,
    for they cannot walk.
Do not be afraid of them,
    for they cannot do evil,
    nor is it in them to do good. (Jer 10:4–5)

One is sure to notice that the idols are marked consistently by lavish gold and silver to decorate them, and so exhibit extravagant

RESISTING DENIAL, REFUSING DESPAIR

wealth (see 1 Kgs 6:1–22; 7:48–50). Thus the object of worship becomes attractive commodity that invites measuring worth by the value of commodity. Such religion has within it the seed of reducing life to a *transactional commoditization.*

On the other hand, however, in a trajectory of much more severe rhetoric, Israel also urges that idols should be violently destroyed because they are seductive and lead Israel away from trust in and obedience to the one true God:

> But this is how you must deal with them; break down their altars, smash their pillars, hew down their sacred poles, and burn their idols with fire. (Deut 7:5)

> The images of their gods you shall burn with fire. Do not covet the silver or gold that is on them and take it for yourself, because you could be ensnared by it; for it is abhorrent to your God. (Deut 7:25; see Nah 1:14)

The reasoning is the same here as with Paul. The idols have *no substantive reality.* But they can be a *dangerous seduction in actual social life and* therefore must be eliminated, even if violently.

— The idols are an *affront* to serious faith and to serious relational life.

— The idols are a *distraction* because they siphon off resources that are elsewhere better deployed.

— The idols are *divisive* because they cause the community to choose up sides in a dispute that is about nothing substantive.

— The idols are a *distortion* of reality that diminishes common sense and skews our capacity to see the world as it is under the rule of God.

Thus in both the Old Testament and Paul we see a *total theological rejection* of idols and an *acute sociopolitical awareness* of the toxic practice of idolatry that does damage to the community.

So now among us, we are witnessing social conflict over the removal and destruction (or maintenance) of statues of Robert E. Lee, Andrew Jackson, and their company that have been erected to specify white domination and supremacy long after the Civil War was finished. The destruction of the statues is fueled by a claim that they convey (and are intended to convey) white supremacy in a way that skews reality. The defenders of the statues anemically insist that they are only memorials to a troubled but treasured history. But surely Jim Wallis has it right:

> Many white people are learning what Black people already know: that the white knee on a Black neck is a system, a culture, a false idol, and a brutal violence that permeates every aspect of American life and structures.[1]

The statues celebrate those who fought in defense of slavery and against the Union. It is not to be missed that the defense of slavery was adherence to an economy that depended upon cheap labor for the sake of a life of comfort and leisure without labor, that is, a defense of a monopoly of gold and silver (not unlike the gold and silver of ancient idols) and the easy life it made possible. Thus, we might notice the nice linkage of *idols-idle* life without labor. There is no doubt that in a quite practical way the statues do indeed *affront, distract, divide,* and *distort* our social life, advocating an economy that required an unequal interplay of masters and slaves. We could not be surprised that those with bodily memory of slavery should find these statues unbearable for what they not only remember but what they continue to evoke.

— These statues are an *affront* because they attest white domination and supremacy over Blacks, a domination that after the war was expressed as indentured servitude made legal.

— These statues are a *distraction* from the real issues of racial justice and equality to which our society is committed in our deepest claims.

— These statues are a source of deep *divisiveness* between those who continue (via the ideology of MAGA) to hope for a restoration of the good old white days, and those who yearn for an enactment of "the better angels of our nature."

1. Wallis, "Virus of White Supremacy."

— These statues are a *distortion* of social reality because white racist ideology still tacitly imagines that it is possible to convert "humans into the totally compliant, submissive, accepting chattels symbolized by Aristotle's ideal of the 'natural slave.'"[2] Of course it is not put that way, but every effort at keeping Blacks from just equality is a step toward that implied but unexpressed brutalizing goal.

Most benignly these idols of racist domination should not be fed the "meat" of devotion, honor, or protection. Rather on a quite practical level the "strong" who claim these statues are not racist should desist from offering "meat" that is affrontive to the "weak" who find them so offensive. In our present moment, however, those who are "strong" in Paul's sense insist on offering "meat" that deliberately escalates the offense of the idols. Indeed, our former president has become the point person for offering "red meat" to "white idols" by the means of inflammatory rhetoric that appeals to his white "base." Such "red meat" appeals, by design, to the *basest* impulses of the *base*.

When the "strong" will not or cannot stop the "red meat" offered to "white idols," according to the rhetoric of the Bible, they must be "hewn down." They might be hewn down by the vigorous passion of those most offended. Or they might be hewn down by the wise action of government. Either way, they must be hewn down. The statues as idols still do not have any substantive reality, "because no idol in the world really exists." But they nonetheless skew social reality. It is no stretch to see that the destruction of the idols is a proper service to make room for the rule of the true God of justice, mercy, and truth.

2. Davis, *Problem of Slavery*, xiii.

6

REFUSING THE BRAMBLE

I HAVE DELIBERATELY WAITED until after the election to make the following expository comment. I have waited because I did not want such a rich text to be "used up" by the election. The poetic probe in Judg 9:8–15 is situated in the book of Judges amid a sustained contestation about public leadership. The book of Judges consists in a series of disconnected "hero stories" that have been secondarily connected by a strong, highly visible editorial hand. In these hero stories themselves, in each case an uncredentialed leader has arisen to deal with oppression and to accomplish emancipation for the Israelite tribes from an exploitative adversary. These several leaders exhibit brashness and boldness, courage and ruthlessness, and so accomplish victories over Israel's enemies that warrant great celebration in Israel.

The follow-up in each case of such victory and emancipation is that the hero lingers in power as "a judge" for an extended period of time. There are no established protocols or institutions of power in Israel, but there is will for sustained stable leadership (something like a king!). These heroes, moreover, are not reluctant to take such power when it is offered to them. These "judges" regularly give Israel safety and security ("rest") for extended periods that consists in freedom from external threat. Thus, the "rest" after

Othniel was for forty years (3:11), after Ehud, eighty years (3:30), after Barak and Deborah, forty years (5:31), and after Gideon, forty years (8:28). The highly stylized reportage of the book of Judges discloses an urge toward a more stable form of leadership that hovers over the book of Judges. Israel yearns for a king! In a little noticed but surely important book, John C. Yoder has suggested that the nearest parallel we have in our contemporary world to the book of Judges is "the pervasiveness and perseverance of patron-client politics in Africa."[1] In that culture, a strong man arises who provides stability and social continuity and order of a durable kind. In a practical bargain, the client-subjects willingly provide support and taxation to sustain such an order. This is what we see in the book of Judges.

Such an arrangement, however, generates a wish for something more durable, that is, kingship. After the refusal of kingship by Gideon (8:23), in the next narrative Abimelech has no such reluctance and seizes power as a king. He does so by the murder of his seventy brothers who might have been a threat to him (9:1–5). Amid the massacre, one of his brothers, Jotham, escaped, "for he hid himself" (9:5). Jotham, the lone survivor, of course sees the danger of such absolutism; in the text that claims our attention here, Jotham issues a parabolic warning to Israel from the top of Mount Gerizim at Shechem. Thus the narrative of Abimelech (9:1–57) is interrupted by the poetic parable that intends to counter the menace of Abimelech's absolutism (vv. 8–15).

The poetic parable of Jotham imagines a nominating committee of the trees to designate someone to be king, to "hold sway" over all the trees. Of course, such a committee would seek only the best and strongest nominees. In this case of the trees (that is, all plants) the best and strongest nominees are an *olive tree, a fig tree,* and a *vine.* These are the most luxurious and desirable crops of Israel's fertile land. It is interesting that the conventional triad, "grain, wine, and oil" is modified with "fig tree" instead of "grain," perhaps because a fig tree produces edible fruit, or perhaps because

1. Yoder, *Power and Politics in the Book of Judges.*

"grain" would not qualify as a tree. In typical folklore fashion, we get three candidates, not more, not less.

Each of the three nominees makes the same brief speech in order to decline the post of ruler. Each of the three claims to be engaged in the production of rich food and is unwilling to interrupt that good work for the sake of governance. This triad of excuses is perhaps an anticipation of the three excuse-makers in the parable of Luke 14:18–20. Each of those three is too busy and otherwise engaged to be interrupted by an invitation to the banquet.

Two matters may be observed about these excuses in the parable. First, each excuse takes the trouble to state the spectacular wonder of the present work of food production. Thus:

— The olive tree: "my rich oil by which gods and mortals are honored" (v. 9).

— The fig tree: "my sweetness and my delicious fruit" (v. 11).

— The vine: "My wine that cheers gods and mortals" (v. 13).

The point of such lavish descriptions is to insist how wonderfully urgent is the work and to expect that even the nominating committee would surely not want to disrupt that good work.

Second, the poetic formulation of declination is in Hebrew quite terse:

— Olive tree: shall I cease my fatness of oil?

— Fig tree: shall I cease my sweetness?

— Vine: shall I cease my new wine?

Only the third mentions the actual produce; the others employ only descriptive adjectives. In each case the point is the desirability of the fruit. And in each case the question anticipates that even the nominating committee would answer, "No, of course you should not desist from your productive work."

These statements that refuse election are elliptical. English translation requires the verb "produce" that is lacking in the Hebrew. But the point is that these plants are engaged in useful production that should not be interrupted by political engagement.

This sentiment is readily reiterated in our contemporary commitment to production and commoditization! Don't disturb useful production!

When these three most attractive tree-candidates are removed from the field, space is left for the fourth candidate, the "bramble." (This is quite an unusual word in the Old Testament, used only elsewhere in Ps 58:10 with reference to a thornbush used for fire wood.) The bramble is thorny, unattractive, and menacing. In the parable, the bramble is eagerly ready for governance. The bramble makes a speech promising to provide protective shade. But the bramble requires "good faith" (*emeth*), that is, a reliable commitment from the other plants. That is, the bramble asks for a blank check of allegiance. That promise of protective shade, however, is accompanied by a threat of devouring fire that would engulf even the great cedar trees. One can sense that this speech of acceptance by the bramble is laden with ominous potential.

That speech in the parable, moreover, is closely matched by the speech concerning Abimelech in the narrative of vv. 19–20 that also bids for "good faith" (*emeth*) for Abimelech, and also offers a threat of devouring fire. This candidacy is indeed "playing with fire"! Thus, the parable has an eye on the narrative (or the other way round) and wants to call attention to the onerous offer of governance by Abimelech. And there the parable ends. It does not report that the rule of the bramble is accepted by the other trees. It leaves open the response that must be made by those who hear the parable, that is, by those who face the governance of Abimelech. This parable, like every parable, requires the listeners to complete the parable by deciding upon a response. In the narrative, we are not told that the rule of Abimelech was accepted, only that he lasted in power for three years, while his brother, Jotham, who has told the parable, "ran away and fled . . . for fear of his brother Abimelech" (v. 21).

The point of the parable is not obscure. The parable is simply a clever way to assert that if good people with positive political potential default on governing responsibility, then rule will be exercised by less desirable, more dangerous alternatives. The point is clear; nonetheless there is merit in lining out the parable. Not only is it entertaining in its imagery, but the repetition of patterned speech reinforces the danger and the possibility concerning governance. In the case of this narrative, the parable implies that Abimelech came to power because better candidates refused to have their productive lives interrupted by public responsibility.

It takes no great imagination for us to see the contemporaneity of the parable for us. If responsible people eschew public responsibility, the way is open for "lowlifes" to occupy governing space. I have wanted to wait with this parable until after the election because I did not want it to be taken simply as an invitation to vote in the election. That would be minimal. The point I wish to make is that the parable pertains to public engagement between elections, that is, all the time. Public life is a day-to-day enterprise. Many good, responsible people (like me!) exercise our "political franchise" at election time and then relax until the next election. But the "brambles" of dark money and nefarious hidden money-power never rest or take a day off from seeking leverage, advantage, and control of the public apparatus. That everyday engagement cannot be resisted or countered simply by voting. It can only be countered or resisted by regular insistent engagement in the "down ballot" work of organization, money, vigilance, and effort all of the time.

Our recent political experience has made clear that our political institutions and traditions go by default to the brambles if they are not defended and performed with faithfulness. Thus the work of pastoral leadership, I suggest, is to show how, why, and in what ways political engagement by ordinary citizen-believers is part of our urgent vocation. This will require sustained pastoral intentionality in order to counter and resist the usual assumptions among us that pastoral work is exclusively private, one-on-one, and spiritual with a disregard of public issues. Faith pertains exactly to public power, public money, and the common good. There is no reason that a local congregation should not be an engine for political energy that is committed to the practice of compassion, mercy, and restorative justice in the public domain. That practice is not conservative or progressive, Republican or Democratic. It is rather about the love of the neighbor by the shape and energy of public will. An urgent pastoral task is surely to refocus faithful energy toward public life so that the brambles do not carry the day.

The long sorry narrative of Abimelech ends with an uncompromising theological flourish:

> When the Israelite saw that Abimelech was dead, they all went home. Thus God repaid Abimelech for the crime he committed against his father in killing his seventy brothers; and God also made all the wickedness of the people of Shechem fall back on their heads, and on them came the curse of Jotham son of Jerubbaal. (vv. 55–57)

In this concluding resolve of the narrative, it is affirmed that political exploitation and self-serving violence cannot finally outflank the good governance of God. Or as Senator Sam Irwin said during the Watergate investigation, "What you sow, you will reap." Indeed! "They all went home." We may hope they all went home to continuing public engagement. Unless, of course, they had not learned anything. If they had not learned anything from the devastating episode of Abimelech about the fragility of common life, then there was likely more to come of political violence that would further jeopardize the safety and the prosperity of the body politic.

7

SHAMELESS NORMALITY

JEREMIAH OFFERED A SCATHING assessment of the ruling oligarchy that governed ancient Jerusalem that included king, priests, scribes, and prophets:

> From the least to the greatest of them,
>   everyone is greedy for unjust gain;
> and from prophet to priest,
>   everyone deals falsely.
> They have treated the wound of my people carelessly,
>   saying "Peace, peace,"
>   when there is no peace.
> They acted shamefully, they committed abomination;
>   yet they were not ashamed,
>   they did not know how to blush. (Jer 6:13–15)

These fierce words of the poet were so on point and poignant that they are reiterated by the editors of his book yet again:

> From the least to the greatest
>   everyone is greedy for unjust gain;
> from prophet to priest,
>   everyone deals falsely.
> They have treated the wound of my people carelessly,
>   saying "Peace, peace,"
>   when there is no peace.

> They acted shamefully, they committed abomination;
>   yet they were not at all ashamed,
>   they did not know how to blush. (8:10–12)

Jeremiah was able to see clearly the abject failure of public leadership in Jerusalem that was not visible to those safely contained in the ideology of Davidic election. Those so contained only believed in "making Israel great again."

Jeremiah saw clearly:

1. He saw that the primary principle of public life in the city was *unmitigated greed* that was generated in a desperate sense of self-sufficiency. He saw that the organs of state, temple, and the law were all distorted for private gain at the cost of public well-being. He saw that the city's economic enterprise was grounded in ideology-propelled exploitation.

2. He saw that such willful distortion of public life and the public economy required wholesale deception and the *issuance of fake news* in the service of an ideology that was remote from economic reality. Thus the propaganda of throne and temple issued *false mantras of assurance* that were misleading and misrepresenting of social reality. Those false mantras of assurance seduced much of the population of the city.

3. Before he finished, Jeremiah saw that the force of ideology had been able to establish in Jerusalem a new social narrative that offered a triad of unregulated greed, phony press releases, and willful misrepresentation that should have embarrassed the perpetrators of such distortion. The leadership—priests, prophets, scribes, however, had *lost any capacity for shame.* They could no longer be embarrassed by their gross acts and policies. They had lost their ability to blush, because their grossness had achieved the status of the new normal. Greed and misrepresentation were perfectly fine: "We do it all the time and everyone does it." No problem! When long-held social expectations and constraints can be violated with impunity, the capacity for shame evaporates. That is what happened in Jerusalem. There were no longer any tacit constraints to which the leadership was accountable. The loss of shame, says

Jeremiah, leads to a devastating "therefore" from which the leadership will not be exempt:

> *Therefore* they shall fall among those who fall;
>   at the time that I punish them, they shall be overthrown,
>   says the LORD. (Jer 6:15; see 8:12)

In the latter text the prophet introduced his scathing assessment with another ominous "therefore":

> *Therefore* I will give their wives to others
>   and their fields to conquerors. (8:10)

Shamelessness leads to disaster!

It requires little imagination to transfer this loss of social restraint from that ancient city to our present social reality. In our contemporary social crisis:

1. *Greed reigns*! There was a time when the controlling oligarchs in our society had to act covertly. Not now! Now it is all out in the open: regressive taxation, cancelation of food stamps, bailouts for corporations coupled with reduction of Medicaid coverage, the firing of discomforting inspectors general and the termination of constitutional oversight, deployment of federal moneys in partisan ways, all without cover-up and without apology. The grasping of greed by the powerful has become normative in law and nobody blinks at it anymore.

2. *Phony reassurances* are the order of the day, assurances that have no basis in fact:

— "America is back," when clearly the economic crisis has not been addressed, and racism goes its unfettered way

— "A victory lap" over the virus when the toll of deaths expands, in many places unchecked

— A full and recovered economy is certain "by the fall," when in fact recovery will be slow and cautious with much economic pain still to come

— A ready capacity to "go it alone" when in fact the United States needs the international community to face effectively the realities that are coming in terms of health and the environment.

These phony assurances are offered in a ready eagerness, without empathy or compassion, to dismiss unbearable socioeconomic reality that is all around us. The assurances are unblinking and finally shameless in their cynicism!

3. These practices of greed and these offers of phony assurances among us are without restraint. Their perpetrators are *unchecked by any sense of embarrassment.* They echo the lines of Mayor Richard J. Daley, who famously said amid a scandal, "Nothing embarrasses us." When the capacity for shame evaporates, the maintenance of human dignity and the valuing of human life are dramatically diminished. Human persons easily become throwaway objects, completely dispensable for those who have reduced life to tradable commodities.

For such brutalizing practice and policy everything depends upon the verification of new normals that no longer seem stunningly abnormal:

— It is a new normal among us that homeless persons, that is, the house-disadvantaged, are accepted as ordinary social fixtures without hope or reprieve.

— It is a new normal among us that health care is primarily for the well-financed and the well-connected.

— It is a new normal among us that many people should work for pay that make a viable life impossible.

— It is a new normal among us that union-busted labor should have no clout or say concerning rates, terms, or conditions of employment.

— It is a new normal among us that the old racist residues of slavery continue to be forcefully practiced in law enforcement and the administration of justice.

— It is a new normal among us to accept voter repression and gerrymandering that preclude full participation in the democratic process.

— It is a new normal to keep unwelcome children in detention, if not in cages.

All of this is old stuff; but now these practices have become normal and accepted; we are no longer shocked or horrified by the cynical legitimacy of these hard habits. No one is embarrassed. No one blushes. Many of us can remember the dramatic moment when Joseph Welch, the pixie-like attorney, put the question to Senator Joe McCarthy: "Have you, at long last, no shame, Senator?" There was a long pause in that moment; the question was unanswered. It lingered in the air; but the answer was (and is) unmistakable:

— *No*, Senator McCarthy had no shame.

— *No*, the urban elite in old Jerusalem had no shame.

— *No*, the greedy oligarchs among us have no shame.

In the midst of these shameless new normals, God dispatched Jeremiah as a truth-teller. In the midst of our contemporary shameless new normals, God has sent the church. The church is not a nag or a nanny to monitor such policy and conduct.

It is, however, I submit, the proper work of the church (and its pastors) to bear witness to the normals that are ordained of God and structured into the creation that cannot for long be outflanked or violated with impunity:

— *It is normal* that greed should be curbed by an awareness that we live most elementally by gift.

— *It is normal* that every human person should have good housing.

— *It is normal* that every human person should have adequate health care.

— *It is normal* that those who work should receive a living wage and enjoy the fruit of their labor.

— *It is normal* that the wealth of the community should be deployed for the well-being of the neighborhood.

— *It is normal* that the truth shall be told about the deployment of public moneys, about the degradation of the environment, about the index of suffering caused by injustice and inequity.

— *It is normal* that those who violate these norms will be shamed and embarrassed enough to blush.

We live in a society where destructive abnormalities have been recast as normal. But the truth must be told. All those who follow in the wake of Jeremiah are charged with such truth-telling so that we do not, in our drowsiness, fail to see the reality of our world. As Jeremiah discovered, the perpetrators of phony normals do not want such truth-telling. We do it, nonetheless, because we know that the will of God is not finally negotiable. When we do our work well, we may embrace the good charge made to Timothy:

> Do your best to present yourself to God as one approved by him, a worker who has *no need to be ashamed*, rightly explaining the word of truth. (2 Tim 2:15)

8

SQUIRMING TOWARD NEWNESS

Psalm 114 is a lyrical rendering of Israel's exodus memory. The psalm readily divides into three parts, just right for a sermon sketch! Verses 1–2 quickly summarize the master narrative of Israel's faith. That narrative begins with the departure from Egypt and culminates in arrival into the promised land. Here, as in the Song of Moses (Exod 15:1–18), emancipation from Pharaoh ends in "God's sanctuary," that is, in Mt. Zion in the Jerusalem temple. Exodus is not only deliverance *from* (Pharaoh); it is also deliverance *to* safe secure life in the land of well-being at the center of which is the sovereign presence of YHWH in the Jerusalem temple.

After these summary verses, vv. 3–4 engage in a bit of mocking, liberating fun at the expense of God's creatures that are destabilized by the force of the creator God. Verses 3–4 report on what happened at the exodus. "The sea," embodiment of the force of chaos, took one look at the emancipatory resolve of God and fled for safety. That is, the waters retreated in order to make way for YHWH's emancipatory act (see Exod 14:21–22). But here the retreat of the waters is not only for emancipation. The chaotic waters are frightened by YHWH and flee the scene. They are unable to stand in the face of that dangerous holy sovereignty. In poetic parallel the mountains, the great reliable monuments of stability, are reduced to the tottering of newborn lambs that can scarcely stand. Even the mountains that have been there forever become unstable in the face of the emancipatory force of YHWH (see Ps 46:2–3). All creation will desperately yield to the liberating purpose of YHWH, either in fear or in obedience. Thus the exodus is parsed not only as a *historical event* (which it is!), but a *cosmic disruption* of the form and shape of creation. (See Josh 10:12–13, where we have notice of the way in which creation acts for the sake of YHWH's particular intent.)

The rhetorical questions of vv. 5–6 that follow the report of vv. 3–4 constitute a mocking tease. These are rhetorical questions because the psalmist knows very well why the sea and the mountains have fled in fear. Israel, confident of YHWH's liberating intent, says to the restless sea and to the staggering mountains: "Fraidy-cat, fraidy-cat!" They fled because the force of the creator is immense and cannot be withstood. Nothing in all creation can stand in the way of the emancipatory resolve of the creator God. To withstand that resolve is to invite ruin on one's self. The questions of vv. 5–6 are likely an anticipation of the mocking Paul does of the power of death, affirming that death, like chaos, is no match for the God of emancipatory impulse:

> Where, O death, is your victory?
> Where, O death, is your sting?
> (1 Cor 15:55; see Hos 13:14)

Like chaos, death has no sting and no power when assaulted by the God of life. Taken benignly, this mocking affirmation may be taken as "He's got the whole world in his hands," or "This is my father's world." The tone here, however, is not benign. This is a contest to see who will have the final say in creation. It turns out that the sea (chaos) has no final say. Death has no final say.

The final say belongs, without much contestation, to the creator God, a lesson that the forces of chaos and death always have to learn yet again. That is why the God of the exodus could assure the escaping slaves:

> Do not be afraid, stand firm, and see the deliverance that
> the LORD will accomplish for you today; for the Egyp-
> tians whom you see today you shall never see again. The
> LORD will fight for you, and you have only to keep still.
> (Exod 14:13–14)

We are able to hear an echo of this assurance in the mighty affirmation of Paul in Rom 8:37–39!

> We are more than conquerors through him who loved
> us. For I am convinced that neither death, nor life, or an-
> gels, nor rulers, nor things present, nor things to come,
> nor height, nor depth, nor anything else in all creation
> will be able to separate us from the love of God in Christ
> Jesus our Lord.

All of this is from the outset on the horizon of this water-from-
rock God.

Third, the psalm moves to the startling imperative of v. 7
that is no doubt the pivot of the psalm toward which all these
poetic lines have been moving. It turns out that this reference to
the exodus is not simply a history lesson. Rather it is memory that
yields a very present-tense warning. The verb "tremble" bespeaks
the twisting anguish that happens both in the birth process and
in troubled fear and in writhing pain. Thus we may translate it as
"squirm": squirming discomfort in fear or alarm. The imperative is
addressed to Pharaoh as one might expect; Pharaoh should rightly
squirm in fear before YHWH. Beyond Pharaoh, the mandate to
squirm is addressed is to all historical players, all the earthly princ-
es, all the political managers, all the economic predators, all the
authoritarian teachers. Squirm at *loss*; squirm at *embarrassment*;
squirm because *the rule of YHWH* outflanks and undoes all of our
arrangements that serve our comfort, security, and advantage.

And, says the psalmist, if you do not believe that, take a look
back to Exod 17:1–7 and the water drawn from flint rock. Everyone knows, in that prescientific world, that you cannot get *water
from rock*. But we are witnesses to it! We have witnessed creation at
the behest of the creator. We have witnessed the capacity of God to
upend all of our assumptions and all of our power arrangements,

and all of our designations of privilege. Good reason to twist and squirm! The psalmist might also have alluded to *bread from heaven* (Exod 16:14-15) *and quail from the seashore* (Exod 16:13). Or we might be offered an inventory of inexplicable inversions through which the blind see, lepers are cleansed, the deaf hear, the lame walk, and the poor have good news (see Luke 7:22). YHWH is the master of many transformations that the world judges to be impossible. We may be able to notice that the world, under the sway of YHWH, turns out to be very different from that which we had imagined.

Given the breathtaking force of the imperative of the psalm, it is an easy move to the gospel reading in Matthew 18. In that parable the king is accustomed to settling his accounts on time. He is familiar with debt and expects debts owed him to be promptly repaid. He is calling in all his loans. He is a tough dealer who is comfortable with a transactional mode of communication without apology and has a capacity to enforce his transactional demands.

Except—of course the parable concerns a very different governance . . . "the kingdom of heaven" (Matt 18:23). The king in the parable is a practitioner of generosity. He readily forgives debts. He intends that such generosity should pervade his regime. He is sternly impatient with underlings who contradict his generosity. He poses the obvious question to his recalcitrant slave who failed in debt forgiveness: Should you not have had *mercy* on your fellow slave, as I had *mercy* on you (v. 33)? The obvious answer is "yes"; yes, the one who received generosity from the king is expected to replicate that generosity in their own lives and their own claims. Now the king is provoked and insists that his unforgiving slave should be held fully accountable (v. 34). The conclusion of the parable in v. 33 is a severe warning about being parsimonious and deficient in forgiving generosity.

The warning can be taken as an echo of the imperative of our psalm: Tremble! *Tremble* when you contradict the way of the new governance. *Tremble* if you hold on to old parsimony. *Tremble* if you stay inside old transactional calculations. *Tremble* if you refuse the new rule of neighborliness. Such generosity concerning real economic matters is like water from rock. It makes possible real life in an arid economy. It turns out that the parable is about forgiveness of debts . . . real forgiveness of real debts, not the clichés of piety. The kingdom of heaven is about the failure of old transactional systems of social relationships. Debt is the governance of the old order. Debt lasts forever and keeps people in hock and in hopelessness.[1] And now the new governance breaks the vicious cycle!

Debt lingers with its power to disable. Except . . . of course except . . . *the water-from-rock God* wills otherwise. Good news to the indebted. Good news to those too long kept poor and powerless. In Ps 114:1–2 we have seen the quick tracing of our master narrative from Egypt (a place of hopeless debt!) to the new land of well-being. Between *Egypt* and *the new land* is *Sinai*. Sinai is the venue for torah as an alternative to the predatory rules of Pharaoh. This alternative turns on love of God and love of neighbor. It is the exodus God who gives the new torah provision for neighborliness (Exod 20:1). Eventually Moses will extend Sinai mandates to the forgiveness and cancellation of debts (Deut 15:1–18). YHWH wills a new regime of neighborliness. No wonder we are summoned to "tremble"! No wonder we are warned against not showing mercy when we have received mercy.

Just now in our society we are facing the exposé of the long-term debt incurred against Blacks who have worked to "make America great" without pay for a long time.[2] We are now reckoning with the questions of whose life matters. It turns out that the lives of the *debtors* matter along with the lives of the *creditors*. Who knew? Biblical interpreters have a chance to lay out this reality that culminates in an uncompromising imperative. A trembling turn toward the new governance will indeed be as life-giving as water from rock! This is the God who terminated the bondage-making, debt-urging regime of Pharaoh. That remembered deliverance was not and will not be the last time this water-from-rock God acts in mercy. As that happens yet again, we are invited to notice . . . and to tremble!

1. See Graeber, *Debt: The First 5000 Years.*
2. Baptist, *The Half Has Never Been Told.*

9

THE BUGABOO OF "SOCIALISM"

CONSIDER THESE TWO PROPOSITIONS:

1. *Sloganeering is designed to stop critical thinking.* It is a clever device whereby seriously complex matters are made overly simplistic. Such a practice of sloganeering serves, almost always, to "enliven the base" of those who accept the slogan.

2. *Economic sloganeering in our society is completely predictable and equally unhelpful.* On the one hand, economic sloganeering in our society imagines that "capitalism" is a virtuous economic enterprise that is beyond fault or critique. This mantra permits the celebration of "rugged individualism," the "free market," and the illusion of "the self-made man." It fosters, moreover, the illusion that anyone who is smart and hustles can succeed to wealth and the privileges it brings. On the other hand, our usual sloganeering makes "socialism" (an ill-defined and slippery term) the great bugaboo for everything bad from authoritarianism to free love to child abuse. With the convenient juxtaposition of "virtuous capitalism" and "evil socialism," there is of course no critical thinking.

Critical thinking, by contrast, requires us going behind and beneath the simplistic reductionism of slogans to the complexities of real life. When we begin to do that, we discover that "capitalism" is not as singularly virtuous as we had been led to believe. We are watching now before our very eyes as cronyism invites the wealthy and well-connected to line up at the trough of public funds. The old and long-standing grants to the oil industry and agribusiness, for example, are not much reported or noted. But we know enough to know that capitalism is not the free-trade idyll as is imagined. And now the rush of tariffs that stacks the cards on behalf of some favorites at the expense of others makes clear that capitalism is not an innocent exchange of goods because there are too many heavy hands on the scale of inequity.

Conversely, the great bugaboo of "socialism" reflects the deep alarm that "someone will get something for nothing," meaning of course, that the poor and disadvantaged will get something for nothing as do the well-connected in oil and agribusiness. One of my lunch partners is an old (nearly as old as I am!) conservative who regularly rails about "something for nothing." His zeal concerning "something for nothing" is about the "lazy indigent" who do no work, even while he has not yet computed that his own evident wealth is a legacy of a slave-owning family that was a long-standing arrangement of wealth for those who did not work, a perfect embodiment of "something for nothing." We have been observing this as a "bailout" in which any hint of "socialism" must be carefully avoided. But the bailout is exactly the use of public funds for the protection of private wealth. Mitch McConnell calls it "an investment." Former Secretary Steven Mnuchin characterized it as "particular assistance at specific points." It is indeed a bailout of selective proportion, but none dare call it socialism!

The church's chance is to go below the slogans to the economic realities. On the one hand, the work of the church is to *unmask* the misleading inadequacy of the slogans. Thus "capitalism" is not, in our current practice, free trade; it is rather the management and manipulation of the economy on behalf of the wealthy and the powerful. Thus "socialism," in our current practice, is not a free handout to "welfare queens," but a diversion of public moneys to benefit those already privileged. But the more important work, on the other hand, is the focus on the inescapable public realities of bodily life, namely, *health, education, housing,* and *jobs*. Focus on these bodily realities gives the lie to most of our treasured slogans:

Health is a requirement for a viable human life. It is a task the community undertakes on behalf of every member of the community. Thus the church's question for the public discussion might be:

Which neighbor do you think should not have health care?

Education of the ongoing task every community undertakes. In addition to learning the skills to earn a living, every community has a stake in a child learning life skills to be able to participate in the political processes of the community. In the end, the debate about private or public schools is a false issue. The real issue is whether we will have children who grow up with a historical awareness of the wonder and obligations of citizenship. So we may put the question:

The child of which neighbor do you think should be denied an education that is as good, responsible, and well-funded as the education of every other child?

Safe, secure *housing* is a requirement for viable living. We talk flippantly about "the homeless," as though that population were a "different breed," of course readily "a lesser breed." In fact, "the homeless" are those who lack adequate housing. So we pose the question:

Which neighbor do you think should not have adequate secure housing?

Jobs in a dog-eat-dog economy are conditioned by a great class divide. Children of privilege grow up without ever experiencing the reality of disciplined labor. And the need of a steady supply of immigrants to do the hard work at low pay is evidence of the loss of dignity and respect for serious work. In the midst of the economic slowdown and unbearable unemployment, we have at the same time an urgent need for immigrants to do the hard work. We are left with the question:

Which neighbors should work for low pay?

Or how can it be that some work not at all and enjoy privilege and advantage, while others must work endlessly in order to survive? How might that be redressed? It is the case, moreover, that to some very great extent the wealthy who manage the economy are in fact not producers of anything. Roland Boer has seen that already in ancient Israel the economic question was:

How does one enable the nonproducing ruling class to maintain the life to which its members had quickly become accustomed?[1]

What a combination: "*ruling . . . nonproducing*"!!

Of course, dear reader, you have always known all of this, all about the "big four" of *health, education, housing,* and *jobs.* But the point is an important one. It is not only the identification of the "big four" of health, education, housing, and jobs. It is:

Neighbor health

Neighbor education

Neighbor housing

Neighbor jobs!

Which neighbor? It comes down to choices that are not unlike *Sophie's Choice* in William Styron's narrative in which Sophie had to decide which child would perish and which one would live in the context of the death camps. When we go below the surface of slogans to the economic realities of daily life, the force of the slogans evaporates. The real question is how to mobilize the resources of the community for all of the neighbors. While "capitalism" and "socialism" are modern constructs, the issues are very old. It is possible to have capitalism that is *greedy or neighborly*; it is possible to have socialism that is *greedy or neighborly*. Thus it is proper to transpose the context of the slogans into a matter of *greed* and *neighborliness.*

The prophet of Israel well understood the destructive force of a predatory economy that took the form of monopoly of property:

> Ah, you who join house to house,
>> who add field to field,
> until there is room for no one but you,
>> and you are left to live alone in the midst of the land!
> (Isa 5:8)

1. Boer, *Sacred Economy*, 203.

The predatory economic capacity to join "field to field" and "house to house" is of course doable. It is always, however, at the expense of the neighbor. The prophetic anticipation is that such accumulation will soon or late become sustainable. Verse 10 is perhaps a polemic against something like agribusiness. When the land is used and not loved, it will simply refuse to produce:

> For ten acres of vineyard shall yield one bath,
>   and a homer of seed will yield a mere ephah.
>   (Isa 5:10)

Such greed is unsustainable because it violates the ordering of creation that cannot finally be outflanked. Of the "vineyards" and "seed" in this oracle, D. N. Premnath has observed:

> It is noteworthy that verse 10 lists two of the major items of export from Palestine: wine and grain. These items were exported in exchange for luxury and strategic military items. Thus, the local economic resources went to support the elite and their lifestyle. The primary producers benefitted in no way from the fruit of their labor. The firm control of the distributive process by the ruling elite was responsible for this. The judgment speaks of depriving the rich of the very things of which they had deprived the peasants.[2]

The contrast between *greed* and *neighborly justice* is central to the work of Jeremiah. The prophet offers a scathing critique of the greedy policies of King Jehoiakim (Shallum):

> Woe to him who builds his house by unrighteousness
>   and his upper rooms by injustice;
> who makes his neighbors work for nothing,
>   and does not give them their wages. (Jer 22:13)

Jeremiah knew about "wages theft." That predatory king is contrasted with his father, King Josiah:

> Did not your father eat and drink
>   and do justice and righteousness? . . .

---

2. Premnath, *Eighth Century Prophets*, 102.

> He judged the cause of the poor and needy
>> then it was well for him. (Jer 22:15–16)

"Justice and righteousness" are not just convenient slogans. They are actual practices through which the "poor and needy" are able to participate fully in the wealth of the royal apparatus. The royal psalm makes such a policy of "justice and righteousness" a precondition for a proper economy and a stable reign:

> Give the king your justice, O God,
>> and your righteousness to a king's son . . .
> May he defend the cause of the poor of the people,
>> and give deliverance to the needy,
>> and crush the oppressor. (Ps 72:1, 4)

The *bookkeepers* in ancient Israel are kept honest by such *poets.* But when the poets are not lively, brave, and insistent, the bookkeepers will come to think that the greedy pursuit of wealth is the only avenue for a safe, good life. That conclusion, however, is only possible when the poets are cowed or silenced. When the poets refuse to be silenced, matters are very different for the economy. The poets make a different critical conversation not only possible but inescapable.

The church (and its pastors) have no stake in the slogans, that is, no special investment in "capitalism" or "socialism." The concern of the church is singularly *the neighbor* and *the neighborhood.* The "neighbor" is the only theme in economic matters that is relevant for the church. We have known this since Moses:

> You shall love your *neighbor* as yourself. I am the LORD.
> (Lev 19:18)

We have known this since Jesus:

> You shall love your *neighbor* as yourself. (Mark 12:31)

We have known this since Paul:

> For the whole law is summed up in a single commandment: "You shall love your *neighbor* as yourself."
> (Gal 5:14)

That leaves only the question,

"Who is my neighbor?" (Luke 10:29)

The Bible is unflinching and unambiguous in its identification of the neighbor: widow, orphan, immigrant, the poor, lepers, the blind, deaf, lame . . . all those without viable resources or reliable advocacy. These are the proper concern of the public economy, not to be obfuscated by our familiar slogans.

"Virus time" is indeed *neighbor time*. We are learning—slowly, locally, and daily—that common resources can indeed be shared generously. Such generous sharing is now not labeled "socialism." It is neighborliness. It is this commonsense sharing of public resources that is the theme of the church concerning economics. But the real test will be when the virus is over. We will have a choice to make: to *return* to our old greedy way of anti-neighborliness? Or to *embrace* in a durable way the sense of neighborliness now so evident? It is the church's task, along with the other poets, to bear witness to this reality that subverts the bookkeepers who in normal times love austerity. The passion for the neighbor puts the gospel in opposition to such austerity. I have no doubt that how we will choose in time to come will depend upon the poets in the prophetic tradition. If the poets become silent or timid, we will rush back to parsimony. But if the poets have courage and imagination, we may choose differently. It is certain that the lips of the poets were not ordained for timidity.

10

THE CODES OF CHOSENNESS

IT WAS AN EASY move to recast the identity of ancient Israel as God's chosen people in the Bible to identify Western whites as God's chosen people. This move was accomplished by an imaginative retelling of the biblical narrative of the "promised land" and "conquest," represented, for example, by the Puritan minister Cotton Mather in his book of 1702, *Magnalia Christi Americana*, translated as *The Glorious Works of Christ in America*.[1] Mather rereads the biblical narrative with Western Whites as the blessed protagonists. It was an easy interpretive move; at the same time it was a deeply pernicious move that has become the basis for a long history of exploitation and violence in the service of rapacious greed.

The conviction that Western whites are God's chosen people is a grounding for white supremacy. And once such chosenness is affirmed, two claims follow:

— Whites are "*normal*" *and normative*. Consequently, anything other than white is abnormal and sub-normal.

— Whites are *entitled* to the most and the best, a claim that has long validated the violent colonialization of the West, the

1. Mather, *Magnalia Christi Americana*.

51

forcible seizure of the land, and the removal of Native Americans and then the enslavement of people of color.

This triad of *chosenness, normal, and entitlement* constitutes the long, painful history of the Western world that has, wherever and whenever possible, been extended to the rest of the world through colonialization, militarism, and imperialism. Thus we can read forward from the chosen people of the Bible to the chosen people of the Western world. We can also, however, read backward from the sorry tale of the Western world to the chosen people in the Bible to see that in both instances a conviction of chosenness creates a sense of monopoly with God and a warrant to seize land violently that is already occupied. Thus the claim of chosenness that pervades the Bible, the history of the West, and quite specifically the history of the United States is everywhere an impetus for brutalizing self-regard that can readily make a claim to divine sanction.

US "domination" (a favorite word of our white-supremicist former president) was already expressed by President Andrew Jackson with his policy of Indian removal. He was elected in 1828 with a platform of "Indian removal today, Indian removal tomorrow, Indian removal forever."[2] It is a slogan familiarly echoed by Governor George Wallace as "segregation today, segregation tomorrow, segregation forever."[3] The same theme was pursued by President Theodore Roosevelt in his expansive American imperialism with his judgment that the peoples of Asia were incapable of governing themselves and needed US presence and governance.[4] As we shall see, that status, warrant, and sanction of chosenness, normativity, and entitlement are carefully guarded, maintained, and legitimated by "protocols of holiness" that we may term "the codes of chosenness."

2. Johnson, *Broken Heart of America*, 48.

3. This was part of Wallace's inauguration speech as governor of Alabama in 1963; see the bibliography for the full-text online.

4. See Bradley, *Imperial Cruise*.

The preacher has as her task the exposé, undoing, and disman-
tling of the deeply held and silently affirmed claims for chosenness
that function as a basis for white supremacy and the derivative
claims of normativity and entitlement. One text to which appeal
may be made in this dangerous and urgent task is the rich narrative in Acts 10. Peter, the lead apostle, is reported to have had
a vision in a trance. Such a vision freely violates and undermines
common assumptions that have immense authority in our wakeful
hours, but are vulnerable and open to assault in our sleep. In his vision Peter was commanded by "a voice," a voice from "elsewhere,"
to eat "four-footed creatures and reptiles and birds," all of which
are prohibited as "unclean" by the holiness codes of Israel. They
are forbidden to the faithful because such "uncleanness" would
jeopardize Israel's access to the holy God. The holiness codes thus
separate Israel from other peoples who might be willing to eat
such creatures that they might not take to be "unclean." Deeply
grounded in Israel's holiness codes, Peter refuses and resists the
command (Acts 10:14). But the voice from elsewhere is insistent:

> The voice said to him again, a second time, "What God
> has made clean, you must not call profane." (Acts 10:25)

The voice insistently commands three times (v. 16)! Peter is commanded to break the holiness codes of his people to which he had
been deeply committed! But Peter is a quick study. The next day
he shares company with a gentile, Cornelius. He declares, perhaps
wistfully:

> You yourself know that it is unlawful for a Jew to associ-
> ate with or to visit a Gentile; but God has shown me that
> I should not call anyone profane or unclean. (v. 28)

He declares his understanding of the mandate from the God of
Israel, a new mandate that deeply displaced his previous life and
opened for him a new vocation and a fresh vision of his life in obedience to God. He readily goes public with the daring implications
of his new understanding:

> I truly understand that God shows no partiality! (v. 34)

This in the face of Jewish chosenness! This in the face of white supremacy! This in the face of US exceptionalism! Peter discerns that the treasured codes of his people have been wrong and must be voided. They have misrepresented God's will for holiness and uncleanness. Peter discerns, in this moment, that he must contradict his education and violate the usual assumptions of his people. In this moment he recognizes that the codes of chosenness cannot be sustained. God wills the full and welcome inclusion of the "unclean" Gentles in the new community of the gospel that is the wave of the future. The mandate of the gospel requires a violation of the old codes!

We preachers might linger over the notion that gentiles are "unclean." The codes by which we whites live, codes that are regularly reiterated by our former president, is that Blacks are "lazy," "sexually dangerous" (rapists!), and above all "unclean." Just now a congressman from Ohio opines that Blacks may get more of the virus "because they do not wash their hands enough." Blacks who are lazy, dangerous, and dirty are on all accounts so unlike whites; because they are so unlike whites, they are abnormal, without any entitlement, and therefore subject to exclusion (redlining!), not "deserving" of good schools, or good housing, or good jobs. It all follows from "chosenness"!

We preachers might linger over the codes that are mostly tacit but nonetheless immensely powerful. The most obvious of such codes is "whites only," and the most familiar of such codes is "We reserve the right to serve . . ." In my growing up in a small town that upheld the codes, my teacher "explained" to me that "Blacks like to live in unpainted houses," and "Blacks are offended to be called 'Mr.' or 'Mrs.'" My teacher, I have no doubt, simply took the codes for granted. The codes then and always seem like givens; they function to maintain and legitimate by regular reiteration in the familiar liturgies of state, church, and market. Because the codes are so closely treasured and so deeply trusted, it takes a risky daring extremity like a *dream* or a *trance* or a *vision* in order to see differently, to see that God is no respecter of persons but is evenhanded to all and not partial, not even to those who claim to be chosen, normative, and entitled.

It will not do for the preacher simply to speak of "equality" or our need to "love each other." The preacher may and can assert that the God of the gospel refuses to be contained in the codes that are enunciated in the name of God. Thus Peter is summoned in a trance to move outside the codes of his people that he had been taught were the "codes of holiness." I have come to think that the narrative in Acts 10 is the most important text for the way in which God breaks open our codes that skew the reality that God would have us live. The inclusion of gentiles into the early church radically changed the nature of the church, its message, and its life.

In the same way serious full inclusion of people of color into our common life changes everything and requires whites to move beyond our comfort zones of control and privilege. God's expansive reach and intent are beyond our preferred chosenness, normality, and entitlement. Peter is a model for the disruption of our comfort zones, as is Paul on his way to Damascus. In this moment the force that breaks the codes of the early church was staggeringly demanding for the church; it opened to the church a vision concerning the new world of God's intent.

When the preacher takes up the code-breaking narrative of Acts 10, she has behind her the Pentecost narrative in Acts 2. In that dazzling moment of the rush of God's spirit, all the old delineations are transgressed:

> Amazed and astonished, they asked, "Are not all these who are speaking Galileans? And how is it that we hear, each of us, in our own language? Parthians, Medes, Elamites, and residents of Mesopotamia, Judea, and Cappadocia, Pontus and Asia, Phrygia and Pamphylia, Egypt and the parts of Libya belonging to Cyrene, and visitors from Rome, both Jews and proselytes, Cretans and Arabs—in our own languages we hear them speaking about God's deeds of power." (Acts 2:8–11)

(Note: The preacher, in reading this paragraph, should not skip any of these names, but sound them all because the effect is cumulative, surely intended by the author to be so). The Spirit does not respect our social arrangements. The vision of Paul and the trance of Peter are instances of the Spirit's work of code-busting. The Spirit that shatters the codes makes a new community possible.

The preacher who lingers with Acts 10 has in front of him the grand vision and anticipation of the coming world that God will bring that will displace the weary empire of Rome and every other human contrivance of deeply coded entitlement. We may for that reason sing a new song:

> . . . from every tribe and language and people and nation
> you have made them to be a kingdom and priests serving
> our God. (Rev 5:9)

The grand inclusiveness of "every tribe, language, people, and nation" is like a recurring mantra in this vision of the coming world (see Rev 7:9; 13:7; 14:6; 17:15). This envisioned world is not to be governed by our codes of fear, but by the self-giving of the Lamb. The result of this lyric is a radically altered human community. It is this reconstituted human community that stands before us as we face a move beyond our racist delineations of human reality.

The preacher, situated in Acts 10 with Pentecost behind her and the coming new world of barrier crossing in front of him, has the hard work of decoding to do. That work includes the discovery that the gentiles are also chosen for participation in normality and entitlement. So among us those excluded by the old codes are now fully participant in the new world of normality and entitlement. It is no wonder that the book of Revelation teems with doxology. The singing of the new world is a powerful echo of the singing of Miriam as the newly freed slaves "saw the Egyptians dead on the seashore" (Exod 14:30). The stubborn adherents to the old codes are left behind!

Now to finish with a poignant note of humor. Joseph Lowry, the great Methodist advocate for social justice who died recently at a ripe age, was once at a sit-in at a lunch counter. Finally, the waitress said to him, "We don't serve colored people." Lowry responded, "I did not order colored people. I ordered chicken salad."

11

JUBILATION FOR A SOJOURNER

THE HEBREW WORD GER is variously translated as "sojourner,"
"immigrant," or "alien." It refers in the Old Testament to a vulnerable population that was without property or property rights,
that lacked social protection and economic resources, and that was
regularly on the move, always to another territory where it was not
welcomed. Sonia Shah writes of such folk:

> Migrants tend to be the kind of people who don't have
> big bank accounts or landholdings or titles but are rich
> in good health, skills, education, and social connections
> with people in other places. Their capital is portable . . .
> They're the kind of people who are the bedrock of suc-
> cessful communities . . . they are healthier, too.[1]

It is odd, but nonetheless true, that such folk may bring with them
what Shah terms "the healthy migrant effect" to a community but
are nevertheless most often taken to be a threat to the established
order.

Give or take a nuance, it is odd but true that Jim Wallis at
Sojourner fits that characterization in remarkable ways. He brings
a good bit of social capital with him that is indeed "portable." He

1. Shah, *Next Great Migration*, 277.

is bedrock for the well-being of his community, and he is, for good reason, often perceived as a threat to established social order. I am glad to salute this "champion sojourner" as he completes fifty years of work and resolved leadership of the *Sojourner* community.

That community was founded in 1971, with Wallis among its leaders, out of Trinity Evangelical Divinity School in Chicago. It emerged at the height of the Vietnam War in the midst of immense social turmoil among us. Originally called "Post-American," it set out to witness against the grain of US nationalism and was something of a commune, which was not so odd in those shrill days. Out of "Post-American" came a community, a magazine, a movement, and Jim Wallis, who would be a faithful, compelling voice for faithful justice in our society for the following fifty years.

Since that founding fifty years ago, Wallis has emerged as a consistent, reliable prophetic voice among us. His remarkable voice is as *truth-teller*, as he unflinchingly bears faithful witness to the ills and evils of our society, notably *America's Original Sin*.[2] His voice is, at the same time, a *hope-teller*. Wallis does not linger excessively over his acute social analysis, but moves regularly and in fresh ways to his summons to action in his conviction that wise public engagement can and will eventuate in a healthy body politic for all of our members.

Wallis, of course, is no conventional progressive whose views are shaped by the liberal opinion of the *New York Times*. After all, he is from Trinity Evangelical and is thoroughly rooted in evangelical faith. Thus he is a throwback to evangelical faith before it was co-opted and distorted by the frightened seizure by the right wing. There was a time in our country when evangelicals were at the forefront of justice issues; Wallis continues to embody that tradition. His urgency about justice matters is not simply a common-sense reality. It is for him all about discipleship and faithfulness to the gospel. Among other things, including editorial work and prophetic leadership, Wallis has over time nurtured a great number of young people into faithful Christian witness, so that they

2. Wallis, *America's Original Sin*.

follow in his train as a great company of those who have inhaled wisdom and courage from him.

Now, after fifty years, Wallis relinquishes leadership of the movement, the community, and the magazine. That good big round number "fifty" attests to Jim's steadfastness in which he has been unwavering in his discipleship and witness. That good big round number, beyond being a measure of his faithfulness, invites us to connect, as Wallis surely would do, to the same good big number in the Bible as the year of the Jubilee.

My guess is that Wallis, as a well-rooted evangelical, first became aware of Jubilee by reading the text of Luke 4:16–20. In that narrative, Jesus is in the synagogue at Nazareth. He reads from the scroll of Isaiah, perhaps an assigned text. The narrative quotes the text Jesus read from Isa 61:1–4 (Luke 4:18–19). The Isaiah text concerns "the year of the LORD's favor," a reference to the Jubilee year. That is the year, so Jesus read, when the Spirit of YHWH extends with anointing empowerment with care for poor people, prisoners, blind people, and oppressed people, that is, all of those excluded from and rejected by a well-ordered society. This remarkable prophetic announcement from Isaiah anticipates the transformative, emancipatory power of God deployed in the world because God wills:

debt cancellation for the poor,

release for prisoners,

restored sight for blind, and

protection for the oppressed.

This is a vision of real social power mobilized on behalf of those who have been victimized by misused social power. In the Lukan version, Jesus then asserts that he himself is the enactor of that prophetic vision. It was this latter claim by Jesus that evoked aggressive hostility against him. His listeners did not mind the notion of Jubilee as long as nobody was active about it.

I was not at Trinity Evangelical when Wallis studied that Gospel reading. But I can imagine that Jim and his classmates with him were dazzled by this gospel text (surely encouraged by good teaching) so that it became an igniting instance for students in 1971 in the United States. The narrative, of course, goes on to show how Jesus claimed his own identity in a Jubilee of debt canceled. That text is enough to set Jim and his cohorts on their way with passion and energy.

Maybe it was a bit later that Wallis pushed back behind Luke 4 to pay close attention to Isaiah 61 that concerns the restoration of devastated Jerusalem. He would have found the same words that Jesus quoted in the synagogue. He would have read about Jubilee:

> To proclaim the year of the LORD's favor,
>   and the day of vengeance of our God. (Isa 61:2)

He would have learned that the text is the dispatch of one who will be at work to restore devastated Israel in the exile. The entire passage is about the promise and expectation of a transformed society:

> Garlands of joy instead of ashes of grief;
>   gladness instead of mourning;
>   clothes of praise instead of a faint spirit. (see v. 3)

All that is tired and sad and worn out is displaced by possibility. The one who speaks these words displays self-identity:

> For I the LORD love justice,
>   I hate robbery and wrong doing . . . (v. 8; see Amos 5:15)

God hates injustice! That must have been a massive moment of learning for Wallis, as for anyone who lingers with this stunning text.

The move back in Wallis's awareness likely continued when he got "learned and sophisticated." He pushed back behind the prophetic oracle of Isaiah 61 to the Torah provision of Leviticus 25 and the Jubilee. In that Torah provision Israel is to proclaim and perform a Jubilee of restoration, the return of property that had been lost in a predatory economy. It turns out, YHWH asserts, that "the land is mine" (v. 24). The land does not belong to economic predators and sharp dealers, nor does it belong to armies of conquest. The land is properly and in perpetuity on loan to small stakeholders who lacked the technical means to protect their property; Wallis also learned that the Jubilee promise is closely echoed in "the year of release" (Deut 15:1–18) in which all debts are cancelled so that poverty may be overcome. These provisions in the trajectory from *Leviticus 25* to *Isaiah 61* to *Luke 4* have provided the leitmotif for Wallis and his brave ministry of witness.

It is worth notice that the word "Jubilee" is from the Hebrew term *ybl* that means "ram's horn." The "ram's horn" was to be blown at the end of forty-nine years to signal the social economic enactment of Jubilee:

> In the year of jubilee you shall return, every one of you, to your property . . . In the jubilee it shall be released, and the property shall be returned . . . They shall serve with you until the year of the jubilee. Then they and their children with them shall be free from your authority; they shall go back to their own family and return to their ancestral property. For they are my servants, whom I brought out of the land of Egypt. They shall not be sold as slaves are sold. (Lev 25:13, 28b, 40b–42)

The sound of the ram's horn in the fiftieth year breaks the vicious cycle of predatory greed that generated poverty and debt slavery. The recovery is restoration to a viable economic life!

I had another thought about Jubilee after fifty years! This year marks the fiftieth year after the founding of what became the Sojourner community. This year marks the fiftieth year of Wallis's leadership of the community. This year marks the year when Wallis relinquishes that leadership to Adam Taylor. This year, then, is a proper time to blow the ram's horn to set in motion exuberant joy and gratitude in celebration for Wallis's steadfast leadership. Jubilee is always a time of joyous celebration, for who does not want debt cancelled or property returned? It is time for such joy for and with Wallis. I imagine that all over our land there is gladness for Jim. I imagine jubilation. We say "jubilate" for Jim and for his fifty years of bold hard work in which he has exhibited faithful discipleship.

I am glad to add my voice in celebrating Jim's fifty years. Happily, it is not a time for his retirement. It is rather a time when he embraces a new career as a full-time teacher: lucky students! It is a new career; it is not, however, a new vocation. I know it is a time for me to voice deep gratitude and equally deep affection for Jim in his obedience to the God of Sinai. The "sojourn" continues through and beyond Jim:

> Yet all these, though they were commended for their faith, did not receive what was promised, since God had provided something better so that they would not, apart from us, be made perfect. (Heb 11:39–40)

Imagine that: All that Jim has done depends on us to bring it to fruition. We must be at that! But for now we may pause to sing, "Jubilate, jubilate, jubilate!" "Jubilate" marks Jim's faith:

> Now our wants and burdens leaving
> To God's care who cares for all,
> Cease we fearing, cease we grieving;
> At God's touch our burdens fall.
> *Jubilate! Jubilate! Jubilate! Amen!*
> Cease we fearing, cease we grieving;
> At God's touch our burdens fall.[3]

---

3. Samuel Longfellow, "Now on Land and Sea Descending," in *Glory to God*, 545.

12

MLK WAS NO HANANIAH

THE PSALMIST ASKS THE question people in trouble characteristically ask in one form or another:

> How long, O LORD? Will you forget me forever?
>   How long will you hide your face from me?
> How long must I bear pain in my soul,
>   and have sorrow in my heart all day long?
> How long shall my enemy be exalted over me? (Ps 13:1–2)

The questions are partly an act of hope, having no doubt that present trouble can and will surely be overcome by God. But these
questions are also an impatient complaint; the trouble has gone
on more than long enough, and it is high time to have it come to
an end. These are the same questions we now have about the virus.
Our question is as well in part an act of hope, as in, "We will get
through this." It is for us as well also a statement of impatience:
this is long enough and we cannot bear it any longer. The questions
require a response, if not from God then from the authorities.

One answer is given to these questions of the psalmist in the
voice of Hananiah, a prophetic figure in Jerusalem after 598 BCE
when the Babylonians had taken from the city the first wave of

deportees. Hananiah—whose name means "Yah is gracious"—answers with a ready assurance:

> Thus says the LORD of hosts, the God of Israel: I have broken the yoke of the king of Babylon. *Within two years* I will bring back to this place all the vessels of the LORD's house, which King Nebuchadnezzar of Babylon took away from this place and carried to Babylon. I will also bring back to this place King Jeconiah son of Jehoiakim of Judah, and all the exiles from Judah who went to Babylon. (Jer 28:2–4)

Hananiah asserts that the deportation will soon be over and all will come home, all 3,023 of them (Jer 52:28)! Perhaps Hananiah has geopolitical reasons for his hope-filled answer. More likely it is a conviction that God, in God's faithful mercy, would not allow such suffering by God's chosen people any longer. But beyond such conviction, it is also the case that Hananiah was closely allied with the royal-priestly establishment of Jerusalem. That establishment had a huge interest in reiterating the absolute control of God over the city, for that absolute divine governance also legitimated crown and throne. Thus Hananiah is not disinterested, but was eager to reflect the political interests of the elite. As a consequence his *theological conviction* is complexly intertwined with *vested interest*. The city establishment wanted and needed a hope-filled answer and Hananiah was ready and able to provide it: a quick return to normalcy!

From the perspective of the book of Jeremiah, Hananiah and his ilk are phonies. They are not dispatched by God (Jer 23:21–22)! They echoed what the establishment wanted:

> From prophet to priest,
>   everyone deals falsely.
> They have treated the wound of my people carelessly,
>   saying, *"Peace, peace,"*
>   *when there is no peace.*
> They acted shamefully,
>   they committed abomination. (Jer 6:13–15)

From prophet to priest
    everyone deals falsely.
They have treated the wound of my people carelessly,
    saying, "*Peace, peace,*"
    when there is no peace.
They acted shamefully,
    they have committed abomination. (Jer 8:1–12a)

They announce peace and well-being that will permit the elite to move past the crisis of deportation quickly and go on with business as usual.

I write this on the day that President Trump is taking a "victory lap" at the Lincoln Memorial, declaring the defeat of the virus. That declaration is in the presence of masses of death and the scientific anticipation of many more to come. His illusionary statement reflects an impatient eagerness to move past the crisis more rapidly than the facts permit in order to return to the normal work of control and money-making. In response to such assurance as that voiced by Hananiah, the prophet Jeremiah is unpersuaded. He insists that there will be displacement for deported Jews in Babylon for a very long time:

For thus says the LORD of hosts, the God of Israel:

I have put an iron yoke on the neck of all these nations so that they may serve King Nebuchadnezzar of Babylon, and they shall indeed serve him: I have even given him the wild animals. (Jer 28:14)

It is as though the King of Babylon is the new Adam, the one in charge of all creation! "The beast" is sent by God and will not be overcome soon!

Faced with brutalizing racial rejection a generation ago, Martin Luther King, in his momentous speech in Montgomery at the end of the Selma march, also gave answer to the inescapable question:

I know you are asking today, "How long will it take?" Somebody's asking, "How long will prejudice blind the visions of men, darkening their understanding, and driving bright-eyed wisdom from her sacred throne?" Somebody's asking, "When will wounded justice, lying prostrate on the streets of Selma and Birmingham and communities all over the South, be lifted from this dust of shame to reign supreme among the children of men?" Somebody's asking, "When will the radiant star of hope be plunged against the nocturnal bosom of this lonely night, plucked from weary souls with chains of fear and manacles of death? How long will justice be crucified and truth bear it?"

King's cadence is not unlike that of the psalmist. It is the old question of faith amid suffering. It is the question in ancient Israel. It was the question in old Montgomery. It is the question in every hot spot of the virus: "How long?" And then King answered:

I come to say to you this afternoon, however difficult the moment, however frustrating the hour, it will not be long, because "truth crushed to the ground will rise again." How long? Not long, because "no lie can live forever." How long? Not long, because "you shall reap what you sow."

And then King added:

How long? Not long, because the arc of the moral universe is long, but it is bent toward justice.[1]

King's "not long" may sound like the "Not long" of Hananiah or Trump. But it is in fact very different. Hananiah anticipated a quick fix, as in, "It will soon miraculously disappear."

King, however, does not engage in magical thinking. He is no Hananiah. He is does not offer any easy assurance. He is not saying anything that will reassure the establishment that wants to get on with business. He knows that faithful living amid crisis (racial crisis or virus) offers no quick fix, but requires moral courage and

1. King, "Remaining Awake through a Great Revolution." See the weblink in the bibliography to the transcript and recorded speech.

brave action. His own life (and death!) attests that his "not long!" was a long, hard, durable piece of hard work.

In our moment of crisis with the virus, we are not to engage in illusions that can only be self-destructive. The granular, quotidian reality of bodily life in history does not admit of magical solutions. We are always facing the *either/or of Hananiah* (with his illusionary expectation) *or King* with his hope-filled realism. In the wake of King, we are called to moral courage for the long haul and brave, durable action that must, perforce, be grounded in truth-telling. We have known this since Jeremiah, even when we wish it were otherwise.

13

NABOTH AGAIN, PART 1

THE STORY OF NABOTH'S vineyard (1 Kings 21) is a towering, uncompromising witness to the pertinence of YHWH to socioeconomic matters. The narrative is so towering and so uncompromising that we may take it as a paradigmatic tale that functions as a lens for the interpretation of many other texts. (I find this paradigmatic witness so important that, following this chapter, I will continue this discussion in the following three chapters.)[1]

The story is located amid the cluster of narratives that feature Elijah and Elisha, two outsized characters who take up a lot of space in Israel's imagination. These stories are set in the midst of the Omri dynasty, a regime in northern Israel that exercised significant power in international politics at the time (876–842 BCE). It is striking that this cluster of narratives concerning these two figures occupies nearly one-third of the entire books of 1 and 2 Kings. They lie outside the domain of the royal regime and reflect a different social location, a different epistemology, and a different socioeconomic passion. They articulate a social reality and a social possibility that lie beyond the control or even understanding of the royal regime.

---

1. See further, Brueggemann, *First and Second Kings*, 257–66.

The plot of the story is quite clear and simple. It concerns Naboth, who owned and cared for a vineyard in the area of Samaria, the capitol city of northern Israel. (We may refer to Isa 5:2 for evidence for how a vineyard was attentively cared for.) Naboth was a small-time property owner who belonged to his land as much as his land belonged to him. He identifies his vineyard as "my ancestral inheritance." The phrase suggests that Naboth's economic horizon was that of tribal Israel, a system of property that antedated the monarchy. (The same notion of ancestral inheritance is operative in the narrative of Jeremiah 32.) Naboth's socioeconomic purview is quite local. He would likely have maintained distance from the royal economy and would have resented any intrusion of that economy into his steady, stable agricultural practice that was modest but adequate for him. Naboth speaks only once in this narrative. When he speaks it is in order to refuse the proposal of King Ahab to trade another property for his vineyard because his vineyard is convenient for the king. His response is terse and to the point (1 Kgs 21:4).

The counter-character to Naboth in this narrative is King Ahab, who is the son of Omri, the second ruler of the dynasty. Because of the capacity of the dynasty to participate in international politics and economics, it is not a surprise that Ahab thinks of property according to the rules of trade. He regards any property, including Naboth's vineyard, as a tradable commodity available for buying and selling. He does not intend to cheat or muscle Naboth, but offers Naboth good value in a trade. It is clear, however, that he has no interest in or appreciation for the ancient tribal assumptions about the land, because such assumptions mean that property cannot be bought and sold; it can only be treasured and cared for.

Thus, the issue is joined between Naboth and Ahab, between peasant farmer and king. But the issue is also joined between two very different notions of property. For Naboth his property is an "inheritance"; for Ahab the same property is a "possession" without familial, historical, or sentimental linkage. From his stance, Naboth has no option but to refuse the offer of the king. He does not hesitate or blink in his refusal to the king. For him the matter is unambiguous, even if the king cannot fathom such refusal. As the story goes, Ahab is powerless before this peasant refusal and can only fall into depression (v. 4).

But then Jezebel, his queen, enters the narrative. We know that Jezebel, a foreign wife (on which see 1 Kgs 11:2), has no commitment to Yahwism and no understanding of covenantal understandings of familial property. We know, moreover, that Jezebel was host to a number of prophets committed to religious traditions other than Yahwism (see 1 Kgs 18:19).

In our narrative Jezebel takes the initiative on behalf of her depressed husband-king, Ahab. The king understands himself to be foiled by Naboth and so is helpless; the queen, however, recognizes no legitimacy in Naboth's claim and has no such compunction. She promptly organizes a conspiracy to frame Naboth on false charges and so to have him stoned as one who "cursed God and the king" (1 Kgs 21:13). When Naboth is murdered by a mob incited by the queen, his property falls to the crown. With the report of Naboth's death, Jezebel tersely dispatches Ahab to seize the property as his own:

> Go, take possession of the vineyard of Naboth the Jezreelite, which he refused to give you for money; for Naboth is not alive, but dead. (v. 15)

Ahab took "possession" of the vineyard. He "possessed" an "inheritance." So now the king's confiscation, made possible by his ruthless queen, gives him the land of ancient tribal inheritance that he has taken in ignoble ways. It is clear that the narrative offers us two notions of property, two systems of economics, one that has *covenantal rootage* that depends upon fidelity, and the other that is *purely commercial* without any linkage to the fabric of society. It is clear here, as everywhere, that the covenantal practice of property is extremely vulnerable to the force of commercial interest and has few ways to effectively resist it. This clash between systems is crucial to the perspective of biblical faith. This pervasive clash between systems serves to make the Bible immediately and relentlessly contemporary, for this clash of covenantal and commercial is everywhere evident among us. Indeed, one can see that much of Israel's torah is designed for resistance to the commoditization of the land. This is unmistakable not least in the tenth commandment of Sinai:

> Neither shall you covet your neighbor's wife. Neither shall you covet your neighbor's house, or field, or male or female slave, or ox, or donkey, or anything that belongs to your neighbor. (Deut 5:21)

The coveting of a neighbor's field is everywhere at work in ancient and contemporary society, and constitutes a key accent of prophetic critique:

> Alas for those who devise wickedness
> and evil deeds on their beds!
> When the morning dawns, they perform it,
> because it is in their power.
> They covet fields and seize them;
> houses, and take them away;
> they oppress householder and house,
> people and their *inheritance*. (Mic 2:1–2)

> Ah, you who join house to house,
> who add field to field,
> until there is room for none but you,
> and you are left to live alone in the midst of
> the land. (Isa 5:8)

The plot of our story is simple. It is, however, made more thick and complex in 1 Kgs 21:17 with the arrival of Elijah in the story. Ahab addresses Elijah as "my enemy" (v. 20). In response, Elijah declares a severe condemnation of Ahab and Jezebel for their seizure of Naboth's life and inheritance:

> I will bring disaster on you; I will consume you, and cut off from Ahab every male, bond or free, in Israel; and I will make your house like the house of Jeroboam son of Nebat and like the house of Baasha son of Ahijah, because you have provoked me to anger and have caused Israel to sin. Also concerning Jezebel, the LORD said, "The dogs shall eat Jezebel within the bounds of Jezreel."

> Anyone belonging to Ahab who dies in the city the dogs
> shall eat; and anyone of his who dies in the country the
> birds of the air shall eat. (vv. 21–24)

(The fact that Elijah mitigates the harsh judgment against Ahab in v. 29 does not detract from the reality of the divine sanction.)

Elijah's dramatic appearance in the story serves to show that the issue between Naboth and Ahab is not mere economics. It is also a theological dispute, as such economic issues always are. Thus we do well to see the connection between this narrative and the dramatic contest of the gods in ch. 18, where Elijah, on behalf of YHWH, triumphs over Baal and the prophets of Baal. When the *land narrative* of ch. 21 and *god narrative* of ch. 18 are brought together, we can see a *god-land* linkage that makes the matter so urgent. Thus YHWH is shown to be the sponsor and advocate of *land as inheritance*, and Baal is seen to be the sponsor and advocate for *land as possession*:

> And "Baal" is "lord" in the sense of owner—the owner
> of the light and power of nature in and under and over
> the earth, and especially of the light and power or the
> nature of man himself . . . Man outside the covenant and
> Word of God is necessarily man fallen and pledged and
> committed to some such Baal.[2]

It is inescapable in the horizon of this narrative that land rights and land responsibilities are deeply linked to a God-relatedness. Thus the "contest at Carmel" between the gods is reiterated in our narrative as the contest between peasant and king, between inheritance and possession. It is no wonder that Elijah is seen to be "my enemy" of the king (21:20), and elsewhere "troubler of Israel" (18:17), because Elijah represents covenantal interests rooted in YHWH that refuse the commoditization of life and property that are rooted in Baalism and practiced by the royal house. Baal is the god of commoditization in which everyone and everything can be bought and sold, used, traded and disposed of, without worth or value beyond its usefulness.

2. Barth, *Church Dogmatics* IV/1, 455.

While Ahab is given something of a reprieve in 21:29, the harsh judgment against the instigating queen, Jezebel (21:23–24), is not modified and is brought to fruition in due course:

> But when they went to bury her, they found no more of her than the skull and the feet and the palms of her hands. When they came back and told him, he said, "This is the word of the LORD, which he spoke by his servant Elijah the Tishbite, 'In the territory of Jezreel the dogs shall eat the flesh of Jezebel; the corpse of Jezebel shall be like dung on the field in the territory of Jezreel, so that no can say, "This is Jezebel."'" (2 Kgs 9:35–37)

The narrative would have us recognize that in the long run the enterprise of the commoditization of the land sponsored by Baal and implemented by Ahab and Jezebel cannot prevail. In the end, it is asserted, the covenantal reality willed by YHWH, enacted by Naboth, and voiced by Elijah will prevail because it is the will of the Lord of the covenant. The narrative is uncompromising in its conviction, even if our lived experience makes it often less clear and convincing than that. That conviction shows up with clarity in the most elemental contest of the gospel:

> There is a remarkable affinity between Baal, the lord and owner, the god of all natural theology who helped Ahab, as it were, in his sleep—but responsibly as an unjust judge and a murderer and a thief—to possess the vineyard of Naboth, and what the New Testament calls "mammon," the "Mammon of unrighteousness . . ." "No man can serve two masters . . . You cannot serve God and mammon . . ." Ahab tried to do this, and his act of aggression against Naboth was the proof that he could not do so. Neither can any of us.[3]

The either/or of Baal or YHWH (1 Kgs 18:21) shows up on the lips of Jesus:

> No one can serve two masters . . . You cannot serve God and wealth. (Matt 6:24; see Luke 16:13)

---

3. Barth, *Church Dogmatics* IV/1, 458.

Much as we might wish otherwise, on this elemental question it cannot be both/and; it is relentlessly either/or.

14

NABOTH AGAIN, PART 2

FROM MY INITIAL EXPOSITION of the story of Naboth's vineyard in the previous chapter, we can retain three important learnings:

1. The narrative concerns a dispute between two systems of land ownership, inheritance and possession.

2. The dispute between land systems is rooted in a dispute between YHWH and Baal. YHWH is the champion of land as inheritance; Baal is the sponsor of land as possession that leads, in turn, to commoditization.

3. This unequal struggle between these two land systems is interrupted by the sharp critical appearance in the story of Elijah, who is a truth-speaker who exposes the unsustainable folly of royal patterns concerning commoditized owners.

On the basis of these learnings, I propose to consider the life and work of Óscar Romero through a reading of *Blood in the Fields: Oscar Romero, Catholic Social Teaching, and Land Reform*, by Matthew Philipp Whelan.[1] (I strongly commend this book to you, dear reader.) In what follows, I intend to read in two directions, so that the Naboth story may illuminate Romero, and so Romero's

1. Whelan, *Blood in the Fields*.

faith and passion may let us read the Naboth story more deeply and knowingly. Romero was an ordained Catholic priest, became bishop of a poor rural diocese (Santiago de Maria) in 1974, and became archbishop in San Salvador in 1977, to be murdered in 1980. His experience in that poor rural diocese was decisive for him as he witnessed the rigged economic system that exploited the peasants and kept them in hopeless debt. A most remarkable fact about Romero is that as a liberation thinker, unlike almost every other prominent liberation theologian, he made no appeal to the economic analysis of Karl Marx. Rather, his critical passion for social justice—and, consequently, land reform—is based singularly on the Bible and the social teaching of the church.

We may identify three major accent points in Romero's social analysis and prophetic witness. These reference points, of course, were triggered for him by his own pastoral experience with a social system that oppressed and terrorized vulnerable peasants who constituted his pastoral charge. That exposure permitted and indeed required him to reconsider biblical and church teaching with a critical awareness that he would not otherwise have had. This is made evident in the fact that prior to that pastoral experience in Santiago de Maria his inclination was conservative with a reluctance about a liberation hermeneutic. All of that was changed for him by the truth on the ground in Santiago de Maria, a truth his faith would not let him deny or disregard.

First, Romero is a theologian. For him the defining claim of biblical faith is that *the earth belongs to the creator God*. It does not belong to greedy human possessors. It all belongs to God, and God intends it for all creatures, that they may together enjoy its abundance. Second, Romero is a baptized, ordained Catholic who is grounded in *Catholic teaching*, most especially its social teaching. This means that he is informed, in his pastoral horizon, by the teaching of Pope Leo XIII (the great pope who responded prophetically to the Industrial Revolution), the teaching of Vatican II, and more recently by the work of John Paul II. Whelan pays attention to the way in which Romero was guided by the encyclical *Gaudium et Spes* from Vatican II:

God intended the earth with everything contained in it
for the use of all human beings and peoples . . . Whatever
forms of property may be, as adapted to the legitimate
institutions of peoples, according to diverse and change-
able circumstances, attention must always be paid to this
universal destination of earthly goods. In using them,
therefore, man should regard the external things that
he legitimately possesses not only as his own, but also as
common in the sense that they should be able to benefit
not only him but also others.[2]

Third, from that it follows that *all things are to be held in common.* The church of course affirms private property; at the same
time, however, the church recognizes that there is also a "social
mortgage" on private property so that the resources of creation are
to serve the common good, and therefore the good of those who
are excluded from the security and well-being of private property.

From these three accent points of *creation, Catholic social
teaching,* and *the common good,* Romero offers an acute social
analysis that led him to focus on "land reform," that is, the redis-
tribution of the land of San Salvador so that immense estates of
property would be divided to give access to land to those who are
left dangerously exposed and vulnerable. Romero's social analysis
included the following points:

1. Propelling the unjust distribution of the land is *"the idolatry of wealth and property."* It is an idolatry that has led to
   widespread *latifundialism* through which the economic elite
   engage in *geophagia,* that is, "the eating of the earth," and the
   devouring of everything and everyone in the land with an
   insatiable appetite.

2. Such idolatry in turn has produced *institutional violence* that
   is the root of all other violences. The large landowners control
   the instruments of power and policy, and so could enact their
   uncurbed greed in policies and institutions before which the
   landless are vulnerable and helpless.

---

2. Whelan, *Blood in the Fields,* 66.

3. The greed of the ownership class has caused food *production to be distorted and skewed*. No longer is agriculture designed to provide food for subsistence peasants in society as heretofore, food such as maize, corn, sorghum, and rice. Now food is designed for export (and so profit)! That means primarily coffee. When agriculture serves primarily export for profit, there is less food for the indigenous population.

4. The development and maintenance of policies of greed has resulted in *laws of "enclosure"* that fence off property so that the poor can no longer forage in the land. As a result the landless have become more and more dependent upon the economy of the great estates, reduced to "wage labor," and subject to intense and hopeless debt. The loss of access has produced a large population for which political-economic agency is denied.

5. The outcome of such extravagant wealth has eventuated in a careless *"throw-away" culture* of waste and self-indulgence. And of course a practice of "throw away" has meant that landless people are also "left-overs" to be disregarded, thus denying the elemental reality of a commonly shared life including both haves and have-nots.

This convergence of social facts evoked Romero's singular passion for land reform. He understood most clearly that without access to land and its resources the landless people can have no value in a throw-away economy of greed and violence. It was Romero's witness, based on his acute social analysis, that led to his murder.

It should be evident then that Romero, in his witness and passion, reiterates the narrative of Naboth. It is easy enough to see that the agricultural peasants in San Salvador play the part of Naboth, and that the greedy landowners assume the role of Ahab and Jezebel. Like that ancient king and queen, the landowners worship a god of ruthless greed and entitlement. Romero, moreover, is surely cast in the role of Elijah, surely the voice that the landowners would define as "my enemy." We already know from that old story that the acquisition of land by the greedy will readily evoke whatever actions are necessary for the acquisition. It is clear enough to read the story forward to Romero to see that such ruthless greed, in prophetic horizon, cannot go uncurbed. Like Elijah, Romero speaks against the greed on behalf of the creator God who intends that the land should be treasured as a common inheritance and not debased as a fungible possession.

Thus Micah after Elijah, in his condemnation of such destructive greed, anticipates a new division of the land (at the behest of the Assyrians) that will exclude the greedy:

> Now, I am devising against this family an evil
>   from which you cannot remove your necks;
> and you shall not walk haughtily,
>   for it will be an evil time.
> On that day they shall take up a taunt song against you,
>   and wail with bitter lamentation,
> and say, "We are utterly ruined;
>   the LORD alters the inheritance of my people;
> how he removes it from me!
>   Among our captors he parcels out our fields."
> Therefore you will have no one to cast the line by lot
>   in the assembly of the LORD. (Mic 2:3–5)

This later poet anticipates the displacement of exile and the reassignment of land that excludes the greedy owners. This is indeed "land reform" from the top! This poetic anticipation goes beyond the specificity of Elijah; the trajectory in any case is the same. Greedy ownership will, soon or late, be curbed by the intent of the creator God who ultimately governs the land.

It is equally compelling to read backward from Romero to Naboth. When we do that, we sense that the Naboth narrative is no one-off incidental transaction. This is rather a window into the systemic practices that pervaded ancient Israel. The urban elites in the capitol cities of Samaria and Jerusalem depended on the produce of subsistence peasants. Such inequity of *surplus and subsistence* is not sustainable in the long run. It is not sustainable for practical reasons because cheap labor will tolerate exploitation only so long; but it is also unsustainable because the creator of the land will not tolerate such injustice. The reduction of the land to a fungible commodity is sure to bring big trouble on society from which the owners will be able to claim no exemption.

Thus we may be grateful for the life and witness of Romero and, at the same time, appreciative of the narrative of Naboth as we ourselves live in an economy where the gap between haves and have-nots grows daily. The gap is everywhere among us, supported by (1) the idolatry of wealth and property, (2) institutional violence of policing, tax codes, and rigged financial arrangements, (3) food from agribusiness designed for export and profit, (4) privatization of public land to the exclusion of the landless, and (5) a throw-away culture of extravagance that is ready to dispose of unneeded folk as well as other commodities to the great detriment of the environment. Given this evident economic reality now as then, it is urgent that the church learn to reread its text in more knowing, compelling, and courageous ways that are appropriate to the urgency of the moment that God has entrusted to us.

15

NABOTH AGAIN, PART 3

ON THE BASIS OF the learning from Parts 1 and 2 of the story of Naboth's vineyard ("Naboth Again, Part 1"), I want to reflect on a book by Fred Pearce, *The Land Grabbers*.[1] (I commend this book as well to you). The question of who owns the land is an urgent one among us even as it is an ancient question. As early as King David in the Old Testament, the question is posed by Abner, the general who led the forces of Saul who posed a threat to King David. He puts the question directly to the king:

> To whom does the land belong? (2 Sam 3:12)

I take the question by Abner to be a mocking challenge to the king: "So you are a king; act like one and claim the land!" It was an old practice that kings could preempt property from others according to their own will and whim (see 2 Sam 10:9–10). The contemporary mode of that practice is that those with money and power characteristically can have property that belongs to others, whether by paying huge irresistible prices (gentrification!) or by "eminent domain" or other legal acts. Land tends to gravitate toward those who have socioeconomic, political leverage. Who knew?

1. Pearce, *Land Grabbers*.

The gist of Pearce's book is that he traces a most remarkable contemporary economic reality whereby nation-states that lack adequate food resources are in the process of buying up the land of others and using it to produce food that is exported back to the home state. This practice is most prevalent among the oil-rich states of the Persian Gulf. The leader among those states who have money but lack food resources is Saudi Arabia. The Saudis tried to grow food and operate dairies in their desert land, but it was too expensive and required too much of the available limited ground water. As an alternative the Saudis turned to Africa and have bought up huge tracts of land for food production to be exported for the Saudi population. And of course, because the Saudis are rich in oil they have the resources to offer extravagant prices for land that local leaders in Africa cannot resist.

The outcome of such a policy is at least twofold. On the one hand, the practices of local agriculture are disrupted. As more food is produced for export, less food is available for the local population. On the other hand, the urgency of production means that the land is exploited and overused and thereby depleted, thus in contradiction to traditional farming methods that allowed the land its normal processes of recovery and restoration. Consequently, the land grabbers may secure food, but they do so at an enormous cost for the indigenous population and for the land. It is a clear case of land as *possession* and not as *inheritance*. The example of the Saudis is reiterated by many other cases that Pearce fully documents. In practice, the old question of Abner to David is given: the land belongs to those who have means and resources. Those who have long occupied the land are profoundly vulnerable to the pressure of such demand (as vulnerable as Naboth!) and are without means to resist or to protect their land.

I suggest that we may pause, in light of the Naboth narrative, to reflect on the "land grabbers" who have skewed the political economy. Ahab, in the narrative, is such a land grabber. To be sure, he only wanted land for a "vegetable garden" (1 Kgs 21:3). The assumption of Jezebel (and derivatively of Ahab), however, is that they could have possessed much more of Naboth's land, as much as they wanted, by the privilege of the royal office. Ahab grabbed only a little, but Naboth would be helpless if the king had grabbed a lot more of his inheritance.

We may reflect, for a moment, on two well-known and dramatic land grabs. The first is the coming of white Europeans to the New World of the Americas. While the arrival of white Europeans in the Americas is a complex narrative that admits of many "explanations," the simple fact is that it was a moment in which to seize, occupy, and possess land that was long occupied by others. Long behind that historic land grab that gave it important impetus is the papal decree of 1493 called "The Doctrine of Discovery." That papal declaration handed the new world over to Spain and gave Spanish adventurers and the Spanish government the right to occupy the land and to possess its resources, and the freedom to either convert the "natives" to Christianity or to kill them if they did not conform. The "doctrine" assumed that a land that is "discovered" by Europeans could be occupied and possessed, with permission to dispose, as is necessary, of the extant population. While the "doctrine" is very ancient and pertained only to Spain, in practice it was soon generalized to apply to all Europeans in their colonizing reach. By the 1820s, moreover, the "doctrine" was written, by the Supreme Court, into US jurisprudence that became the basis for the aggressive "removal" policies of President Andrew Jackson. The "Doctrine," alas, remains technically in effect even today! The outcome of the action of the land grabbers was a genocide in the United States, all on the basis that white Europeans who occupied the land had entitlement to the land by "discovery" and could remove present inhabitants as necessary either by death or by relocation. The notion of US exceptionalism, already articulated by Cotton Mather, provided the ideological grounds for the policies and actions of the land grabbers, all made religiously legitimate and resounding with patriotic piety. That ideology of exceptionalism made appeal and reference to the great land grab of the Bible that has echoed in subsequent legitimacy.

Second, as a basis for the legitimacy of the white European land grab, the biblical narrative of the book of Joshua has provided theological grist and grounds for such action by Europeans in the New World. In the Bible (as in the biblical commentary of Cotton Mather), the narrative of the land grab is given theological foundation as the performance of the promise of God. Thus in the Bible, behind the book of Joshua is the promise to Abraham and his heirs of a new land given by God:

> Go from your country and your kindred and your father's house to the land I will show you. (Gen 12:1)

> To your descendants I give this land, from the river of Egypt to the great river, the Euphrates, the land of the Kenites, the Kenizzites, the Kadmonites, the Hittites, the Perizzites, the Raphaim, the Amorites, the Canaanites, and Girgashites, and the Jebusites. (15:18–21)

> And I will give to you and to your offspring after you, the land where you are now an alien, all the land of Canaan, for a perpetual holding; and I will be their God. (17:8)

The articulation of "Greater Israel" is traced out in the promise of Genesis 15. That articulation is one that continues to haunt the contemporary state of Israel with its dream of a "greater israel." The promise to Abraham affirms that the land is *a gift given by God* to Abraham's family. By the time of the book of Joshua, of course, what is *given* now must be *taken*, so that the promise is transposed in the text to an effective land grab. The Bible is never able to reconcile the generosity of what is *given* to the forcibleness of what is *taken*, any more than Americans can reconcile *the discovery* of the new land with *the violent disposal* of earlier "Americans."

In her recent, brilliant commentary on the book of Joshua, Carolyn Sharp meets the issue of genocide in that book head on:

> Joshua is a genocidal and colonizing text. What drives the plot is the project of the Israelite army taking territory from the indigenous Canaanite inhabitants, killing or enslaving them as necessary for Israel to establish permanent control of the material resources and political spaces represented by the regions of Canaan. The book of Joshua proclaims the rightness of militarized

colonization, grounding its inevitability and blessedness in God's purposes and enacting genocidal warfare in its narratology at the level of character development, discourse, and plot. Within Joshua, we read a justification designed to overcome the implied audience's horror at the planned annihilation of indigenous noncombatants.[2]

We must acknowledge the violence prompted by means of the coercive rhetoric of Joshua, nearly as pervasive as the violence of events narrated in chapter after chapter. Throughout the book, it is claimed over and over again that to be faithful, the covenant people must give themselves, fully and unflinchingly, to the ideology of militarized colonization and the merciless extermination of indigenous peoples. Those who support the genocidal ideology are portrayed as glorious heroes, as is the case with Joshua and Caleb.[3]

It is clear that land grabbing is at the heart of the biblical narrative (whatever may be historical reality), even while it is given eager theological justification. There is no doubt, moreover, that the land grabbing of the book of Joshua became a warrant for the land grabbing of white Europeans, not only in America, but in New Zealand and Australia as well. The cry for *Lebensraum*, made familiar to us by Hitler, is a very old cry that is a deeply ingrained in the modern world and our US place with it. Along with "living space," land is essential for a secure food supply. Thus in her analysis of the expansion of Charlemagne in the eighth–ninth centuries, Janet Nelson comments: "The state that inspired him [Charlemagne] was the Christian Roman Empire; a very large state that depended crucially, like all empires, on management of food supplies."[4]

Modern states like Saudi Arabia simply continue the practice to do what they deem necessary to assure a reliable food supply, including grabbing the land of others. In the lore of my German

2. Sharp, *Joshua*, 44.

3. Sharp, *Joshua*, 53.

4. Nelson, *King and Emperor*; see also Scott, *Against the Grain*.

antecedents coming to the new world, there is a report of a letter that an early German immigrant, Duden, wrote back to Germany; in the letter he urged immigration to the new world, precisely to Missouri, because the land was so fertile that one can "grow two potato crops in one season." Talk about a secure food supply! In many cases of that requirement of *new land for more food*, acquisition requires wholesale violence. In the case of my antecedents in the new land, this featured systemic violence against Native Americans.

In light of the tradition of aggression for the sake of land and food now being pursued by modern nation-states, Pearce turns his attention to the traditional peasant alternative to such aggressive land grabbing in the pursuit of food. His contention is that traditional farming done by agricultural peasants is the most productive of food and the most generative of good land:

> Smallholder farming is the solution rather than the problem [says Jules Pretty], a success story waiting to happen. Small farms have great potential to increase their output—but also to raise the incomes and improve the livelihoods and skills of their operators.[5]

In one specific case in rural Nigeria, a peasant farmer asserts:

> Crops grow much better with manure . . . I don't use chemical fertilizer at all . . . We can double our yields here easily and improve the environment at the same time.[6]

The contrast between peasant farming and big industrial farming is clear and unambiguous:

> Simple measures of tons of grain per acre may suggest big is best. But small farmers bring many other things to the kitchen table. Official statistics often ignore the fact that they use every corner of their plots, planting kitchen gardens where mechanized farms have vehicle yards. They gather fruits from hedge rows. They have chickens running in the yard. They feed animals on farm waste

5. Pearce, *Land Grabbers*, 301.
6. Pearce, *Land Grabbers*, 299.

and apply the animals' manure to their fields. They raise fish in their flooded paddies. Big farmers may have access to more capital. But ultimately their purpose is to generate returns for that capital—to please their investors, rather than to feed families.[7]

In response, the former president of the Rockefeller Foundation comments:

> [A green revolution] will be driven by smallholders—the 33 million smallholders in Africa with less than two hectares. The people from whom that continent gets 90 percent of its food. It is their productivity that we have to improve.[8]

It is easy enough to ponder this data from Pearce and return to the Naboth story. Let Ahab and Jezebel be a stand-in for big industrial farming while Naboth is a smallholder peasant who treasures his "two hectares" as his inheritance. The contrast is clear among us now as it was clear then. Of course, it is a great leap from Ahab, who only wanted a vegetable garden, to the present aggression of nation-states for food. This is no doubt an over read of the Naboth narrative. But even with his modest claim of Naboth's property, Ahab embodies the reach of Baalism for self-sufficiency that propels the modern states. Thus the Naboth story is a paradigmatic tale that anticipates the contest between two ways of life that now occupies our world economy. The narrative eventually comes to the role of Elijah. Without him, Ahab could have *prevailed* and Naboth would have been readily *forgotten*. So it is among us. Without prophetic alertness marked by courage, the commoditization of land and of people and smallholders will be promptly forgotten. It is the ilk of Elijah who must intervene in order to preclude such *prevailing* and such *forgetting*. Pearce quotes a UN commentator:

---

7. Pearce, *Land Grabbers*, 295.
8. Pearce, *Land Grabbers*, 295.

> There is a cultural prejudice against peasants . . . They are seen as backward, not worthy partners. These ideas are self-fulfilling.[9]

Yet another author could assert:

> The chief scientist's planned revolution stands a good chance of making the poor poorer. Big farms and big investment risk exacerbating the trends that bring hunger amid plenty. We could have both more food and more famines.[10]

Biblical faith has a great stake in the role, identity, and vocation of Naboth. He is the point person for a modest way of life that takes seriously the possibilities and the limits of the land as God's created order. We learn only late and always again that the created order cannot be outflanked with impunity. This is the great nonnegotiable truth voiced by Elijah. No impunity for exploitative pursuit of the land or its "inheritors"! (See Ps 37:11; Matt 5:5.)

9. Pearce, *Land Grabbers*, 293.
10. Pearce, *Land Grabbers*, 293.

16

NABOTH AGAIN, PART 4

IF YOU HAVE FOLLOWED my series of expositions of the Naboth story in the previous three chapters, by now you know the primary accent points of my interpretation. Nonetheless the book by Paul McMahon, *Feeding Frenzy: Land Grabs, Price Spikes, and the World Food Crisis*,[1] merits attention as a rich and suggestive read. (I commend it heartily to you!) McMahon takes a large-scale view of the shape of global food policy and practice and the crisis it has generated. The baseline for thinking about food production is that there was a time when food was *locally* produced, distributed, and consumed. In that practice of food, we can identify the grains that undergirded food usage. In China, it was the "five grains": wheat, rice, millet, soybean, and sorghum.[2] In the West that list would be modified to include potatoes, but the same picture is clear.

The great new fact that has altered the world of food is the capacity to store and export surplus grain. (Naboth of course had nothing like that on his horizon, he being a locally oriented peasant farmer.) James Scott, *Against the Grain*, has traced the way in which the capacity to produce, store, and administer grains

1. McMahon, *Feeding Frenzy*.
2. McMahon, *Feeding Frenzy*, 7.

became the basis of the first great states and empires.[3] (This remarkable development is reflected in the exodus narrative of the Bible that pertains to the slave labor that built the great storehouse cities for the storage of Pharaoh's grain monopoly (Gen 47:13–26; Exod 1:11; 5:4–19). With a long historical leap, McMahon quotes Dan Morgan, who describes "how grain became one of the foundations of the post-war American Empire."[4] This capacity for the storage and export of grain has decisively shifted the reality of food and drawn energy away from local practices of production, distribution, and consumption.

The development of international markets, trade, and export of food caused a great new hunger for land in which farmers were urged to "get big or get out" (Earl Butts, then-secretary of Agriculture). The acquisition of huge tracts of land (that has led to the demise of the "family farm") has been propelled by the profit-making drive of the great food companies:

> Owning and operating farmland is the ultimate form of vertical integration. It allows companies to control every step of the chain from the germination of a seed to the delivery of processed food to the end consumer. The examples given in this chapter are part of a much larger trend of foreign acquisition of farmland, especially in developing countries. Many call them "land grabs." It is the most controversial and dangerous phenomenon to emerge as a result of the recent food crisis, one that has echoes of darker colonial era.[5]

This astonishing land grab has required and evoked a change in the nature of land rights that undermined long-established peasant practices and customs. The new practice has been propelled by profit-seeking agents with whom governmental officials cooperated:

> They target poor developing countries where land is cheap or can be obtained for free. They involve a radical

3. Scott, *Against the Grain.*
4. McMahon, *Feeding Frenzy*, 30; see Morgan, *Merchants of Grain.*
5. McMahon, *Feeding Frenzy*, 178–79.

change in the nature of land rights, usually a transfer from government or local communities to a foreign company in the form of a long-term lease. Host governments are usually heavily involved as they often hold the rights to the land.

. . .

They are often externally imposed by government officials who ignore customary land rights and make massive transfers at the stroke of a pen, or by local chiefs who have been seduced by the investor's chequebook and do not have the best interests of the people at heart. Many foreign investors engage in a sort of sham consultation with local people after the deal has been made—they have no intention of changing their plans.[6]

It takes no imagination at all to see that such vulnerable peasant farmers, not unlike Naboth, have no resources with which to withstand such aggressive economic power. The land grab has been without restraint or limit and is a story of investment for profit:

The investment story presented is usually about buying under-utilized land, investing capital in new seeds, fertilisers, machines or irrigation, and implementing a "modern" high-input, mechanised farming system. This is the sort of narrative financial investors expect to hear, perhaps because it makes farming sound like the industrial sectors they are used to investing in.[7]

It is not at all a surprise, then, that the land (along with its present occupants) has been exploited and abused, over-farmed for the sake of over-production. (Cotton-growing land in the US South is an example of the way in which overproduction has depleted the land as much as it abused those who worked the land. That land now is so impoverished that it can grow nothing other than kudzu.) McMahon describes the way in which land

6. McMahon, *Feeding Frenzy*, 187, 198.
7. McMahon, *Feeding Frenzy*, 258.

degradation and land depletion operate, as the pressure for production and profit override all other concerns:

> A more insidious threat is land degradation. It happens inch by inch, soil particle by soil particle, so slowly that a farmer, like the metaphorical frog in boiling water, is unaware of what is happening until it is too late. Soils can lose their fertility as their composition and structure alter, or they can disappear altogether through the effects of wind or water erosion.[8]

The phrase "soil particle by soil particle" calls to mind the insistence of Wendell Berry, who has said that the recovery of the environment will come, not by some ambitious government program, but rather "one acre at a time." But of course loss of one "soil particle" at a time or the recovery of "one acre at a time" is much too slow and too modest for the great engines of profit.

The insistent and recurring question for those who care is how to develop and fund an alternative policy of production (and land care) that will stop the destruction of the land and interrupt the present economics that has refused sustainable food policy. McMahon nicely identifies the "five processes" that constitute the basis for a farming system: "Selecting plants and animals, managing water, renewing fertility, protecting from pests and applying power."[9] These ingredients of practice and policy are to be kept in purview as we consider how land and food might be cared for and produced in an alternative way. It is not difficult to see how these five processes are factored out by the great "merchants of grain." But the "merchants of grain" characteristically want speed and scale that are unmistakably contrary to both good food production and good land management.

It will not be a surprise that the likely viable alternative to the current profit-driven food policy and practice is a refocus on "small farms" that have been disdained by the "merchants of grain." Thus McMahon concludes:

8. McMahon, *Feeding Frenzy*, 65.
9. McMahon, *Feeding Frenzy*, 9.

An alternative way forward . . . could result in a more benign scenario. Two major themes stand out. The first is the need to help small farmers in poor countries to produce more food. This can kick-start a virtuous cycle of rural and urban development in these countries, while reducing their dependence on rich-country surpluses. The second theme is the importance of switching to agro-ecological farming systems that use fewer non-renewable resources, pollute less and enhance the fertility of the land, while still producing sufficient quantities of food.[10]

There is nothing remote or hidden about these two proposals. They are doable once we are free from the compulsions of scale and speed according to the rhythms of creation. The current global system of food is not working:

The global food system of the early twenty-first century was both impoverishing *and* starving one-eighth of humanity, while leaving an even larger number overweight and at risk of disease. The equilibrium that had emerged was unjust, even perverse. But it was also unstable.

. . .

Many systems of food production are unsustainable. Without change, the global food system will continue to degrade the environment and compromise the world's capacity to produce food in the future, as well as contributing to climate change and the destruction of biodiversity.[11]

This leads McMahon to conclude:

Nothing less is required than a redesign of the whole food system to bring sustainability to the fore.[12]

And then McMahon adds this powerful insight:

10. McMahon, *Feeding Frenzy*, 267.
11. McMahon, *Feeding Frenzy*, 45, 69.
12. McMahon, *Feeding Frenzy*, 69.

> There is a strong economic rationale for placing ecology at the heart of agriculture. Profitability in farming is driven not by high yields but by good margins, the difference between the price a farmer gets and the cost of production.[13]

This is a remarkable and important correction to the uncritical assumption of "food to scale" that high yield is the single goal that matters. McMahon sees that it is not the size of the yield but the margin between cost and price that makes the difference to the farmer. As Berry saw long ago, a highly mechanized farm system requires investment in equipment that is incommensurate with the reality of much farm income. While current commitment to scale, speed, and high yield is endlessly demanding, we may come to our senses with the recognition that food production must soon or late, of necessity, be in sync with the potential, requirements, and limits of the creation as food-giving land. Land as creation has the potential for abundance, but land also has limits; unless and until those limits are acknowledged the potential of abundance is short-term and uncertain. The land as creation has its own requirements that must be heeded. The Promethean technological capacity of our present world food system has assumed that these requirements can be disregarded and outflanked. But we know better than that!

Thus, two conclusions: First: this is, to be sure, a lot to impose on the Naboth narrative. I do so because Naboth serves well as a peasant farmer who wanted only to care for, treasure, and honor his inheritance. It is impossible to imagine that Naboth could care about speed, scale, or high yield. One could imagine, rather, that Naboth would have easily resonated with that other peasant farmer, Micah of Moresheth, the poet, who anticipated a viable local economy outside the arms race of his king:

> But they shall sit under their own vines and their own
>   fig trees,
>   and none shall make them afraid;
>   for the mouth of the LORD of hosts has spoken. (Mic 4:4)

13. McMahon, *Feeding Frenzy*, 258.

(Note well that this verse is missing in the same oracle from the urban prophet, Isaiah [2:2–4].) The additional verse from Micah exhibits the imagination of a peasant farmer who has no inclination for the global food system, but who is content with local food production, the kind that would indeed feed the world.

Second, alternative food policy required for the sake of adequate food and adequate land management is not simply one of a shift of aims. Beyond any shift of resources what is required is an act of imagination that lies beyond the horizon of the great grain merchants. That act of imagination can be evoked by giving voice to peasant wisdom that is local, modest, and frugal in a way that appears from the outside as parsimonious. Peasant wisdom is in deep tension with the insistent advocacies of the technological sector that is variously glib, over-confident, self-indulgent, and excessively self-assured. It is certain that this required act of imagination must come from outside the ideology of scale, speed, and high yield.

It is (surprise!) the work of the faith communities funded by the alternative text of the Bible to seed such counter-imagination. The text entrusted to us is grounded in the claim of God the creator who will not be mocked. This is the God who wills abundance but who keeps the neighbor always in purview, and who intends that creation itself be treated in neighborly ways. At the center of the claim of faith concerning creation is the glad affirmation that the creation, in all its dimensions, belongs to the creator God. A pause in scale, speed, and high yield is essential to the slowdown required for recognition of the creator and of the world as God's creation. It is undoubtedly the case that the practice of local food is in sync with the will of the creator. Naboth understood that in his peasant bones. It is no wonder that the king, committed to scale, speed, and high yield, by the end of the narrative is held under by the severe truth-telling judgment of Elijah. By contrast we may indeed imagine the murdered Naboth joining the song of Francis:

> All creatures of our God and King,
> lift up your voice and with us sing,
> Alleluia, alleluia!

O brother sun with golden beam,
O sister moon with silver gleam . . .
    Alleluia, alleluia!
O brother wind with clouds and rain,
you nurture gifts of fruit and grain,
    Alleluia, alleluia!
O sister water, flowing clear,
make music for our Lord to hear,
    Alleluia, alleluia![14]

The glad utterance of "alleluia" (Praise YHWH!) is a ready recognition of the penultimate status of all creatures, a willingness to be on the receiving end of life, and an acknowledgment of the limits of every Promethean temptation. In that world of glad "alleluia," Ahab's land grabbing cannot finally prevail. In that world, moreover, Naboth will not finally be forgotten or nullified.

14. Francis of Assisi and William H. Draper, "All Creatures of Our God and King," in *Glory to God*, 15.

17

NOT NUMBED INSIDE

My friend Dean Francis loaned me a most remarkable book. Written by John Compton, it is titled *The End of Empathy: Why White Protestants Stopped Loving Their Neighbors.*[1] The book is a carefully researched study about the way in which mainline churches have dramatically lost members and public influence. Compton's research suggests that this has happened to mainline churches because younger church members have fallen away from the social mandates of the gospel and have become preoccupied with individualized matters of self-actualization, self-securing, and self-satisfaction, all pursuits incongruous with love of neighbor. Compton thus refutes the notion that mainline churches have been depleted because they have become "too liberal"; he shows that they were always liberal concerning public issues of justice. Indeed that passion for public issues of justice was largely shared by clergy and lay people . . . until it wasn't! The outcome of this embrace of such individualized goals has led to an indifference to neighbors and thus to a "departure" from the commitments of the "liberal" churches. As a result of what was heretofore taken as a widely shared commitment now has come to be seen as radical

---

1. Compton, *End of Empathy.*

97

and excessively liberal. Compton observes that this "departure" from the church is matched by a more general "departure" in non-church society from the same neighborly values and commitments. This loss of empathy for one's neighbors is a striking and widespread social reality among us.

After reading Compton, I have been thinking about "empathy." The word is an exact etymological equivalent to the word "compassion" that occurs frequently in our English translations of the Bible. Thus:

Em-pathy . . . feeling with;

Com-passion . . . feeling with.

The "death of empathy" concerns the loss of ability or willingness (or both) to "feel with" those who count as "neighbors" in the gospel horizon (see Luke 10:29–37).

The word "compassion" (also rendered as "mercy" and "pity") figures prominently in the Old Testament characterization of God. The word occurs in a strong absolute infinitive in the "credo" self-declaration of YHWH:

The LORD, the LORD,
a God *merciful* and gracious, slow to anger,
and abounding in steadfast love and faithfulness,
keeping steadfast love for the thousandth generation,
forgiving iniquity and transgression and sin . . .
(Exod 34:6–7)

As Nathan Lane, *The Compassionate but Punishing God*, has traced out, the term is reiterated in that credo recital in numerous contexts:

Return to the LORD, your God,
    for he is gracious and *merciful*,
slow to anger and abounding in steadfast love,
    and relents from punishing. (Joel 2:13)

I knew that you are a gracious God and *merciful*, slow to anger, and abounding in steadfast love, and ready to relent from punishing. (Jonah 4:2)

> But you, O Lord, are a God *merciful* and gracious,
> slow to anger and abounding in steadfast love
> and faithfulness. (Ps 86:15)

> The LORD is *merciful* and gracious,
> slow to anger and abounding in steadfast love.
> (Ps 103:8)

> The LORD is gracious and *merciful*,
> slow to anger and abounding in steadfast love.
> The LORD is good to all,
> and his *compassion* is over all that he has made.
> (Ps 145:8–9)

Indeed, we may reckon "compassion" along with "steadfast love" and "faithfulness" as the triad that most marks the readiness of God to "feel with" Israel and with God's; creatures who receive life from God:

> I will take you for my wife forever; I will take you for my wife in righteousness and in justice, in steadfast love, and in *mercy*. I will take you for my wife in faithfulness; and you shall know the LORD. (Hos 2:19–20)

> The steadfast love of the LORD never ceases,
> his *mercies* never come to an end;
> they are new every morning;
> great is your faithfulness. (Lam 3:22–23)

It belongs to YHWH as a God of covenantal faithfulness to be "all in" in solidarity with God's covenant partner. Israel has very little interest in the power of God, though there are ample doxological affirmations of God's power that is taken for granted. What marks YHWH as decisively different from all other gods, however, is YHWH's capacity to "feel with" and "feel for" Israel in the deepest, most intimate ways. That is the reason that Israel's poets must regularly appeal to images of "husband/wife" and "parent/child" in order to portray the passion of this God who knows nothing of "compassion fatigue." In her most remarkable exposition of YHWH's compassion, Phyllis Trible, *God and the Rhetoric of Sexuality*, has shown how the Hebrew word for "compassion" (*rḥm*) is linked to the Hebrew word for "womb" (*rḥm*); both words share the same consonants but with different vowel pointing. Her rendering of Jer 30:20 has these concluding lines:

> Therefore my *womb* trembles for him;
> I will truly show motherly *compassion* upon him,
> Oracle of Yahweh.[2]

With reference to Isa 49:14–15, Trible observes: Heretofore its journey has accented similarities between the *womb* of woman and the *compassion* of God.[3] But YHWH's compassion goes beyond that of a mother. And in Isa 63:15, Trible renders:

> Where are thy zeal and thy might,
> the trembling of thy *womb* and thy *compassion*?[4]

These attestations to the maternal instincts of YHWH signify that there is no end to compassion on the part of YHWH, a capacity that runs even beyond the deep compassion of a mother for her child. The God to whom the gospel bears witness is profoundly and precisely marked by compassion, by a capacity to be stirred internally in solidarity with those in pain and in need.

The work of compassion not only pertains to God; it pertains in an equal way to God's people. Thus Zechariah provides a summary of the covenantal-prophetic mandate to active solidarity:

> Render true judgments, show kindness and *mercy* to one
> another; do not oppress the widow, the orphan, the alien,
> or the poor; and do not devise evil in your hearts against
> one another. (Zech 7:9–10)

In this text the term "mercy" (*rḥm*) is, moreover, in the plural . . . many mercies . . . abundant compassion! We are able to see that covenantal logic insists that God's covenant partner is to be like God: "like God, like people!" The parallel is fully articulated in the twin Psalms 111 and 112. Psalm 111 traces out the character of YHWH:

2. Trible, *God and the Rhetoric of Sexuality*, 45.

3. Trible, *God and the Rhetoric of Sexuality*, 51.

4. Trible, *God and the Rhetoric of Sexuality*, 53.

He has gained renown by his wonderful deeds;
the LORD is gracious and *merciful*. (v. 4)

The psalm then identifies the specificity of YHWH's compassion:

He provides food for those who fear him;
he is ever mindful of his covenant.
He has shown his people the power of his works,
in giving them the inheritance of the nations.
(vv. 5–6; see Deut 10:18)

This affirmation concerning YHWH is matched in Psalm 112 by a sketch of the faithful covenant partners to YHWH:

They rise in the darkness as a light for the upright;
They are gracious, *merciful*, and righteous. (v. 4)

Again, what follows in the psalm details covenantal performance of compassion:

They have distributed freely, they have given to the poor;
their righteousness endures forever;
their horn is exalted in honor. (v. 9)

Compassion is a defining mark of God's people in the world, a community fully committed to the practice of empathy, capable of being "moved" in response to the pain and need of the world. This people is not unlike this God!

Well outside my scholarly competence, I am able to see that it is not different in the gospel narrative of the New Testament. Jesus is portrayed as full of compassion (*splagchnon*):

Moved with *pity*, Jesus stretched out his hand and touched him, and said to him, "I do choose. Be made clean!" (Mark 1:41)

He saw a great crowd; and he had *compassion* for them because they were like sheep without a shepherd; and he began to teach them many things. (Mark 6:34)

I have *compassion* for the crowd, because they have been with me now for three days and have nothing to eat. (Mark 8:2)

> If you are able to do anything, have *pity* on us and heal us. He said to him, "If you are able!"—All things can be done for the one who believes. (Mark 9:22)

Jesus is variously "moved" by lepers, hunger, a possessed child, blindness (and in the parable of Matt 18:27 by poverty). That is, Jesus "feels with" and "feels for" all of those whose humanity is diminished or skewed. He is, moreover, moved by his empathy to effect transformation. The sum of this testimony makes clear (a) that Jesus enacts and performs the *compassion that belongs to the God of the covenant* and, (b) that he enacts and performs the *compassion that belong properly to God's covenant partners*. In Jesus his followers saw for themselves the performance of the empathy of God and the empathy of authentic humanity.

We may go a step further when we observe that the Hebrew word for compassion (*rḥm*) is linked to the term "womb" (*rḥm*), and when we observe that the Greek word for compassion in the New Testament (*splagchnon*) refers to one's "innards" or "entrails." In both usages in both testaments, the term for compassion bespeaks a bodily movement or stirring or disturbance that evokes attention and engagement. That is, compassion is not just a good idea or an ethical resolve. It is, according to these word usages, a bodily response to the pain, hurt, or need of another person, so that there is bodily solidarity from one to another.

Paul appeals to this bodily dimension of solidarity in his characterization of the church as "the body of Christ":

> The members may have the same care for one another. If one member suffers, all suffer together with it; if one member is honored, all rejoice together with it. (1 Cor 12:25–26)

Attention is particularly given to "inferior members," exactly those to whom Jesus was drawn in his bodily solidarity. This reality of solidarity is lined out in the familiar hymn phrase:

> We share each other's woes, our mutual burdens bear; and often for each other flows the sympathizing tear.[5]

5. John Fawcett and Johann G. Nägeli, "Blest Be the Tie That Binds," in *The*

The church, in replication of Jesus and in response to the compassion of God, is a community that exists in and through and for bodily solidarity with the needy and hurting in the world. This is at the heart of the Bible long before we get to policy or to ideology.

It is obvious that our ethical norms and energies are not determined by rational thought. They are, rather, shaped by pre-rational sensibility, that is, by the natural innards of the self. Or to put it directly, we most reliably "go with our gut," even if we dress it up otherwise. What happens in our "innards" shape and propel our engagements in our "outtards," that is, in our social performance. When our innards are open with empathy (compassion) to our neighbors, especially our neighbors in pain or need, we can and will act in ways of solidarity. If, however, our innards are numbed or hollowed out, we likely will act in ways of indifference, without notice of or care for those around us in need or pain. The witness of Scripture is an attestation that the God of the covenant has lively, responsive innards, and so sees the hurt of the world, hears the cries of the pained, and so acts in transformative ways. Indeed, in the memory of Israel that is how the entire enterprise of covenant began:

> God *heard* their groaning, and God *remembered* his covenant with Abraham, Isaac, and Jacob. God *looked upon* the Israelites, and God *took notice* of them. (Exod 2:24–25)

Thus, the God of the gospel is a God of stirred innards who acts with compassion and who, in the agency of Jesus, is "moved to compassion." When we attend to this good news reality, our innards are prepared to engage the reality of the world in transformative ways. When, however, we are engaged with the idols that have no lively innards, we are sure to be increasingly unmoved by and uncaring about the neighborhood around us. Compton traces out the way in which increasing numbers of people have signed on with the idols of self-securing that will never yield lively innards.

United Methodist Hymnbook, 557.

When Israel was in its moment of exilic abandonment, the poet has Israel ask its most pathos-filled question:

> Is it nothing to you, all you who pass by?
>   Look and see
> if there is any sorrow like my sorrow,
>   which was brought upon me
> which the LORD inflicted
>   on the day of his fierce anger. (Lam 1:12)

In its bereft condition Israel wonders if anyone has noticed its plight or taken it seriously. According to Compton's searing analysis, increasing numbers of members of the would-be church answer:

> No, your sorrow is nothing to me;
>
> No, your suffering does not interest me.

That answer, which we may give in our deepest moments of indifference, is reflective of numbed innards. But of course that is not the answer given everywhere. There are many who have answered otherwise:

> Yes, your sorrow is indeed something to me;
>
> Yes, I see and honor your wound.

Those who have such lively innards are an embodiment of the "remnant" of the faithful. In the narrative of Elijah, there were still seven thousand in Israel "who have not bowed their knees to Baal," that is, who have not embraced the gods of numbed innards and unnoticed neighbors (1 Kgs 19:18). This declaration by the Lord contradicted Elijah's mistaken sense that he was the only one left! This is the company that remains capable of empathy and prepared to enact compassion. Thus in every generation, in an echo of Shakespeare (*Henry the Fifth*, act IV, sc. iii), it is "we few, we happy few, we band of sisters and brothers." "Happiness," in context, occurs when we live out the gift of empathy and perform a world of compassion. It is then that we are most fully in sync with the God who gives us life and who entrusts to us lively innards not yet numbed. It is for that reason we sing with joyous gusto when we meet together.

18

ON BECOMING A STATISTIC

THE CARPENTER FROM NAZARETH, Joseph, we may assume, was a modest man who lived a modest life in his village. He did not rock the boat. He did not want to call attention to himself. But then, according to the gospel narrative, he faced two powerful disruptions in his settled life.

The first disruption, according to Matthew, is that the new child of Mary came into Joseph's life. Because he was "righteous" (socially responsible), he was willing to protect this vulnerable mother-to-be:

> Her husband Joseph, being a righteous man and unwilling to expose her to public disgrace, planned to dismiss her quietly. (Matt 1:19)

No wonder he came to be reckoned as a saint! But then he was alerted by the angel from God that this was no ordinary child but one named "Emmanuel":

> But just when he had resolved to do this, an angel of the Lord appeared to him in a dream and said, "Joseph, son of David, do not be afraid to take Mary as your wife, for the child conceived in her is from the Holy Spirit. She

will bear a son, and you are to name him Jesus, for he will save his people from their sins." (Matt 1:20–21)

Joseph was willing and able to render unto God what belonged to God, namely, his honor and his family name. This strange intervention in his life is fully acknowledged in our regular Advent–Christmas observance. It is not now my point of interest.

The second disruption, I suggest, has not been so fully considered for the most part. Imagine the stir in the village of Nazareth the day when a local official posted notice, at the behest of the Jewish government in cooperation with the Roman Empire, that required all inhabitants to be counted in the imperial census. They must do so, moreover, to their great inconvenience in the city of their family. The empire does not mind imposing an inconvenience (more modestly not unlike the scarcity of ballot drop boxes in our recent election)! The posting is reported in the Gospel of Luke:

> In those days a decree went out from Emperor Augustus that all the world [global economy!] should be *registered*. This was the first *registration* and was while Quirinius was governor of Syria. All went to their own town to be *registered*. Joseph also went from the town of Nazareth in Galilee to Judea, to the city of David called Bethlehem, because he was descended from the house and family of David. He went to be *registered* with Mary, to whom he was engaged and who was expecting a child. (Luke 2:1–5)

We may notice in particular two points about this narrative report. First, the report is governed by the term "decree" that in Greek is *dogma*. This is the requirement of the empire, an order well beyond question, debate, or negotiation. It has to be obeyed! It is worth noting that later on, in the book of Acts, some early Christians are described as disobeying an imperial decree:

> These people who have been turning the world upside down have come from here also, and Jason has entertained them as guests. They are all acting contrary to

the decree [*dogma*] of the emperor, saying that there is
another king named Jesus. (Acts 17:6–7)

Such resistance, of course, was not in the horizon of Joseph.
He is willing to render to Caesar what belongs to Caesar, namely,
his money and his political loyalty. Thus Joseph is presented as
being compliant with both interventions. He is responsive to *the
mandate of the angel* concerning Mary. He is equally responsive to
the mandate of the empire that propelled him to Bethlehem.

The second matter we may notice in Luke's report of the imperial decree is that we get four times the term "register":

— All the world shall be *registered* (v. 1).

— This was the first *registration* (v. 2).

— All went to their towns to be *registered* (v. 3).

— He [Joseph] went to be *registered* with Mary (v. 5).

The Greek term for "register" is *apographe* that has within it the
syllable *graph*, thus, "written." The term "register" means to "be
written down," or recorded for all time in the imperial archives.
No resistance to this imperial requirement is noted by Luke as
Joseph willingly complies. We may nevertheless notice that such
an act of being "written down" is likely quite foreign to the village
inhabitants who intended to remain unnoticed and unrecorded.
In their ordinary lives villagers live in an oral world where there
is no need to write things down. It is the special province of the
state to proceed in writing. See two ominous cases of state writing
by Jezebel (1 Kgs 21:8–9) and David (2 Sam 11:14–15). In both
cases the state writing resulted in violent deaths! Thus the requirement of being "written down" recruited Joseph (and Mary) into a
zone of historical reality that was not only new to them, but surely
contrary to their social location and self-identity. Village people
have no inclination to be written down by the empire. A current
extreme case of resistance to being "written down" is the memoir
by Tara Westover, *Educated*, in which Westover details the care her

family took to stay off the "books" and to remain out of reach of the "writing" society.[1]

No protest against the imperial census by Augustus is voiced in Luke's narrative (as Luke has a complex attitude toward Rome). In the older narrative of 2 Samuel 24, however, the census conducted by King David has immense destructive fallout. In that narrative Joab cautiously protests to David about the census suggesting it is unwise: "But why does my lord the king want to do this?" (2 Sam 24:3). It is as though Joab might say to the king, "Why would you want to do such a crazy thing?" Joab nevertheless obeys the king in the implementation of the census. It turns out that the census is judged as an evil for which David receives due punishment. In the escalated account of 1 Chr 21:1–6, the initiation of the census is credited to the pernicious intent of Satan:

> Satan stood up against Israel, and incited David to count
> the people of Israel. (v. 1)

The census can only be an act that intends evil!

Thus we may consider why a state would conduct a census only to know the exact number of inhabitants. While the census in our time has come to serve many other subsidiary purposes, at bottom the census intends to serve only two purposes. On the one hand, it is to establish a clear roster for *taxation*. On the other hand, the census provides data for *manpower resources*, that is, for purposes of military conscription. The state needs only two things from its subjects. The state needs tax money to operate (and to fund surplus ease), and it needs manpower to conduct war. It is undoubtedly true that both needs, tax revenue and manpower, are inimical to a villager who did not want to pay taxes and who surely did want to fight state wars. As a result, in the narrative of 2 Samuel 24 only bad things can come from the conduct of a census:

> Three things I offer you; choose one of them, and I will
> do it to you. So Gad came to David and told him; he
> asked him, "Shall three years of famine come to you on
> your land? Or will you flee three months before your

---

1. Westover, *Educated*.

> foes while they pursue you? Or shall there be three days
> pestilence in your land? Now consider, and decide what
> answer I shall return to the one who sent me." (2 Sam
> 24:12–13)

In the end David chose as his punishment for the census what
he took to be the lightest sentence; and even of that punishment
"the LORD relented concerning the evil" (v. 16). But even as David
is relieved of punishment, the point is clear. A census is an evil,
God-defying act because it permits the state to classify, quantify,
and commandeer its member, even to reach into the most remote
vulnerable villages for state purposes. YHWH, in the Samuel narrative, will have none of it, as David begins to practice statecraft
in a way that his son, Solomon, would carry to self-destructive
extremes. Joseph, however, does not resist the imperial decree. He
docilely obeys (as Luke would have a good Jew do)! In his docile
obedience, nonetheless, Joseph has become an imperial statistic.
He is now numbered among the tax-paying Galileans!

I suggest that in Advent and Christmas we may ponder, on
the one hand, what it was like for Joseph and Mary to be "written
down" by the empire. In the narrative itself, no good comes of it.
King Herod had a list of all the families and all the new babies, that
is, all the new baby boys (Matt 2:16). Joseph and Mary had to flee
from the threat of the state once they had been written down (Matt
2:13–15). It is a dangerous thing to be written down by the state.
We are almost everywhere familiar with undocumented immigrants among us who take great care not to be written down . . . not
to vote, not to claim any reportable income, not to be noticed by
the state. David Graeber, in his daring book on the history of debt,
has observed how peasant revolutions regularly want to storm the
offices and burn tax records; tax records constitute a primary way
in which the state pursues the vulnerable.[2] Thus the destruction
of state files is an act of defiance and emancipation. Once we are
written down, one's name is forever in the unforgiving memory of
the state.

2. Graeber, *Debt.*

On the other hand, we may ponder what it is like to be a state statistic. The state is a quantifier that counts and lists and administers. In our recent election we have seen how campaigns are conducted and propelled on the basis of quantification. Only an occasional media vignette pauses long enough to listen to a potential voter with a specific story. The state has no interest in specific stories. In one very awkward recent campaign episode Donald Trump sought to engage an individual voter in a conversation. It was clear that he had no interest in or energy for the charade in which he participated. The state does not notice that a villager from Nazareth who went to Bethlehem to be "written down" not only has a name (long before being written down) but has a family as well, an occupation, a role in the village, a known identity. So we are back to the old sociological distinction between *Gesellschaft* ("society," "corporation") and *Gemeinschaft* ("community," "partnership"), or in the parlance of Martin Buber, I–It and I–Thou. Joseph has just become an "It" in the Roman system. In our current political climate (and no doubt in ancient Rome), it takes a lot of money to be known by name. All the rest of us are mere statistics!

The purpose of the church in this regard is to refuse to settle for being written down as a statistic, and to insist upon the immediate oral practice of face-to-face contact with all of the distinctiveness of every person . . . every member, every stranger, every street person, every needy person. Thus we provide names in the sacrament of Baptism wherein we commit an act of resistance against any reduction to a statistic. When the priest or pastor says, "What is the name of this child?" something of cosmic significance happens. The new name is uttered; the new person is called into being, blessed, and recognized. That new person, and then every person, is named in a thickness that is occupied by memory and hope, by pain and joy, by fear and possibility.

That no doubt is how Joseph arrived in Bethlehem, filled with memory and hope, with pain and joy, with fear and possibility. None of that mattered, however, to the cynical officials who occupied the village of Bethlehem. They had no interest beyond signing Joseph up as a statistic. David Graeber, *The Utopia of Rules*, characterizes the statistic-producing enterprise and the damage it does to human personhood:

> But the culture of evaluation is if anything even more pervasive in the hypercredentialized world of the professional classes, where audit culture reigns, and nothing is real that cannot be quantified, tabulated, or entered into some interface or quarterly report . . . [The bureaucratic system] begins with the irritating caseworker determining whether you are really poor enough to merit a fee waiver for your children's medicine and ends with men in suits engaged in high-speed trading of bets over how long it will take you to default on your mortgage.[3]

That must have been the atmosphere in Bethlehem. All of that is operative in the innocent-looking narrative of Joseph with the "decree" to be "registered." It turned out that the process of registration was an enemy from which Mary and Joseph had to flee.

It belongs to the church to be a haven for those who fear being "written down." It belongs to the church to gather all of the baptized, but beyond them all of those with names who refuse to become statistics. It is no wonder that Peter later on mustered enough boldness from his community of the named to assert:

> We must obey God rather than any human authority.
> (Acts 5:29)

None of that was on the horizon of Joseph as he made his way to Bethlehem; it was, however, in the purview of the subsequent church in the book of Acts. The church is a statistic-defying community where we are all named, noticed, protected, and nurtured.

We will no doubt continue our Christmas pageants with winged angels who re-perform the angelic intervention into the life of Joseph. We should not, however, neglect the second intervention into the life of Joseph, the way in which the empire (or now the global economy!) seeks to reduce a village peasant to a statistical cipher devoid of identity and denied any viable future. Christmas is a mighty protest against that reductionism. It refuses

3. Graeber, *Utopia of Rules*, 41–42.

the quantitative dismissal of those among us who must be fearful of being written down!

19

ONLY TWO?

WHEN THE HEBREW SLAVES departed Egypt, they all went. They all danced at the border as they were emancipated. They all came into the wilderness. They all ate quail that showed up inscrutably. They all ate the "bread of heaven" and were filled and satisfied. They all drank water from a rock. They all lived according to the new emergence of God's abundance in the wilderness.

When the time came to enter the land of promise, however, the community of the emancipated was sharply divided. The spies who scoped out the new land of promise returned with a report of the luxurious land of milk and honey:

> We came to the land to which you sent us; it flows with milk and honey, and this is its fruit. (Num 13:27)

The fruit they exhibited was extravagant:

> They cut down from there a branch with a single cluster of grapes, and they carried it on a pole between two of them. (v. 23)

The spies, however, added to their report an adversative sobering "yet":

> Yet the people who live in the land are strong, and the
> towns are fortified and very large; and besides, we saw
> the descendants of Anak there. The Amalekites live in
> the land of the Negev, the Hittites, the Jebusites, and the
> Amorites live in the hill country; and the Canaanites live
> by the sea, and along the Jordan. (vv. 28–29)

The good land of promise was already occupied by ferocious, formidable giants!

> So they brought to the Israelites an unfavorable report of
> the land that they had spied out, saying, "The land that
> we have gone through as spies is a land that devours its
> inhabitants; and all the people that we saw in it are of
> great size. There we saw the Nephilim (the Anakites come
> from the Nephilim); and to ourselves we seemed like
> grasshoppers, and so we seemed to them." (vv. 32–33)

The report of the spies voiced a profound tension between lavish
produce and formidable occupants.

It is no wonder that this twofold report evoked conflict in the
community. On the one hand, the *majority opinion* chose to accent
the risk and danger posed by the giant occupants of the land who
contrasted ominously with the self-perceived tiny and vulnerable
grasshoppers of the Israelites. The majority wished for a return to
the good old days. They wanted to make their "slavery great again":

> "Would that we had died in the land of Egypt! Or would
> that we had died in this wilderness! Why is the LORD
> bringing us into the land to fall by the sword? Our wives
> and our little ones will become booty; would it not be
> better for us to go back to Egypt?" So they said to one
> another, "Let us choose a captain, and go back to Egypt."
> (14:2–4)

They were defined by fear that caused them to renege on the land of
promise, ready to resubmit to the old brutal certitudes of Pharaoh.

The *minority report*, to the contrary, did not blink at the
danger of the gigantic occupants of the land, but believed that the
good land (and its good fruit) was to be had because they were the

substance of God's promise. That minority report was issued by Caleb already in 13:30:

> Let us go up at once and occupy it, for we are well able to overcome it.

Caleb spoke with complete confidence against the fear of his companions. And so the die is cast: a *majority opinion grounded in fear*, a *minority opinion rooted in hope*. The issue is sorted out in a divine response to the urgent petition of Moses. His petition to YHWH for mercy is a classic formulation that closely echoes the divine declaration of Exod 34:6–7. Moses prays God's own declaration back to God. In his petition Moses holds YHWH to the earlier self-declaration:

> Let the power of the LORD be great in the way that you promised when you spoke, saying,
>
> > The LORD is slow to anger,
> > > and abounding in steadfast love,
> > forgiving iniquity and transgression,
> > > but by no means clearing the guilty,
> > visiting the iniquity of the parents upon the children
> > > to the third and fourth generations.
> > (Num 14:17–18)

YHWH has provided grounds for forgiveness for the faithfulness of Israel. But YHWH is no easy mark. YHWH weighs in on the contrast of the *majority of fear* and the *minority of hope*:

> None of the people who have seen my glory and the signs that I did in Egypt and in the wilderness, and yet have tempted me these ten times and have not obeyed my voice shall see the land that I swore to give to their ancestors; none of those who despised me shall see it. But my servant Caleb, because he has a different spirit and has followed me wholehearted, I will bring into the land into which he went and his descendant shall possess it. (14:22–24)

Caleb is the first to be named as a candidate for the land of promise. He ranks along with the faithful Joshua:

> Not one of you shall come into the land which I swore
> to settle you except Caleb son of Jephunneh and Joshua
> son of Nun . . . But Joshua son of Nun and Caleb son of
> Jephunneh alone remain alive, of those men who went to
> spy out the land. (vv. 30, 38)

These two will enter the land of promise. These two, no more! Only these two. All the others in their timidity, their backward look, and their lack of trust in God's promise will die in the wilderness:

> Your dead bodies shall fall in this very wilderness; and
> of all your number, included in the census, from twenty
> years old and upward, who have complained against me,
> not one of you shall come into the land in which I swore
> to settle you. (vv. 29–30)

Entry into the land of promise depends on readiness to trust the promise and equal readiness to run great risks for the sake of the promises. The majority played it safe, were unable to trust, and unwilling to risk. They have no future, but only confidence in a past that will no longer function effectively for them. The reliable promise to the two is reiterated:

> Not one of them was left, except Caleb son of Jephunneh
> and Joshua son of Nun. (Num 26:65)

> . . . none except Caleb son of Jephunneh the Kenizzite
> and Joshua son of Nun, for they have unreservedly fol-
> lowed the LORD. (Num 32:12)

> Then Joshua blessed him, and gave Hebron to Caleb son
> of Jephunneh for an inheritance. So Hebron became the
> inheritance of Caleb son of Jephunneh the Kenizzite to
> this day, because he wholeheartedly followed the LORD,
> the God of Israel. (Josh 14:13–14)

The single mark of qualification is "wholeheartedly following" without reservation. Caleb and Joshua are "all in." They were the only two who were all in. All the others in their fearfulness were excluded from the future of abundance in the land of well-being.

Our current crisis of virus and economic meltdown in-vites a rereading of this narrative. The crisis has led us into a wilderness-like context where Pharaoh's certitudes are no longer adequate or persuasive. It is an arena without visible life supports wherein wilderness-like protest and complaint are the order of the day. There is an impetus by the protesters to push toward new social possibility that is no more clear an alternative to us than was the "land of promise" to the erstwhile slaves in the wilderness.

We get glimpses of that coming "land of promise" through stunning acts of neighborly generosity, through such surprising gestures as police kneeling with protestors, and through provocative slogans like "Defund the police." It may be that the police-free protest zone in Seattle is a harbinger of an alternative world. One reason to think that the zone is such a harbinger is that it evoked in former President Trump an alarmist conviction that the only thinkable social model is one of police control (domination!). This urge to domination is in the tradition of the slave-drivers of old whose work was to keep people in their proper place and at work (see Exod 5:10–18). The unacceptable alternative, in the fearful horizon of the former president, is an out-of-control defiant laziness! There is also, however, a bold countermove that asserts that we cannot and will not go back there; we must invest our bodies and our lives in the imaginative work of new policies and practices of neighborly generosity.

The old wilderness was a liminal moment with a readiness for the not-yet-in-hand land of promise or the chance to go back to the old brutalities that were pervaded by certitude. Our wilderness-like crisis is just such a liminal moment. The choice between *fear and hope* was a choice then even as it is now. Back then there were only two who hoped, only two! The others were fully inured to the brutal, insatiable ways of Pharaoh. And now ours is a moment like that. Back then there were only two. We do not yet know how many or who will be among us in the current procession of hope. It isn't quite right to slot the old as those who look backward as the young look forward. It is more complex than that. But there is something to that demography, even as I write this at eighty-seven. Ross Douthat, a reliable conservative, has written that the current conservative movement "now [is] a worldview for old people and contrarians."[1] It is in any case clear that the "base" for former President Trump consists mainly in old white males who crave old certitudes and who believe we can promptly return to them. Indeed, the final "A" of "MAGA" is "again" of a racist, patriarchal society with most others left behind as second-class folk. For some that "again" of exclusionary patriarchal predation is the only imaginable comfort zone.

The good news is that there are now more than two who anticipate the coming land of promise. Beyond the wilderness of our crisis the coming "land of promise" will be marked by:

— a practice of *neighborliness* with less greedy individualism;

— an economy of *generosity* with less predatory parsimony;

— a health care system of *hospitality* with less exclusionary privilege; and

— a criminal justice system of *forgiveness* with less vengeful "law and order."

If we take these markings together—*neighborliness, generosity, hospitality, forgiveness*—they sound not unlike what Jesus called "the kingdom of God." Of course, the outcome of our crisis with its attendant protests is not the kingdom of God. It is, nonetheless, a close enough reiteration as to authorize risk and hope. For the implementation we will require new initiatives, a readiness to listen to the "left behind" in order to learn how to proceed and where to come down. Then there were only two. This narrative of Caleb and Joshua continues to ask us, in the cadences sung by Pete Seeger, and written by Florence Reece:

> Come all you good workers
> Good news to you, I'll tell
> Of how the good old union
> Has come here to dwell.
> *Which side are you on?*

Joshua had anticipated Pete and Florence:

---

1. Douthat, "It's Trumps Revolution."

Now if you are unwilling to serve the LORD, choose this day whom you will serve, whether the gods your ancestors served in the region beyond the River or the gods of the Amorites in whose land you are living; but as for me and my household, we will serve the LORD. (Josh 24:15)

No doubt Caleb said the same.

20

IMAGINE—THE APOSTLE PAUL
MEETS FRANCIS BACON!

FRANCIS BACON (1561–1626), ALONG with his contemporary René Descartes, may be reckoned as a pioneer of Enlightenment rationality. Bacon articulated the most elemental principles of modern science. Along with that, however, he concluded that "nature" was an object for study and usefulness, and that human agents are free to make of and take whatever they want of "nature" without restraint. Thus, Cameron Wybrow, *The Bible, Baconianism, and Mastery over Nature*, can conclude:

> The investigation has uncovered two Baconian themes: the penetration of the secrets of nature, and the kinship of this penetration with acts of violence and rape.[1]

(If you, dear reader, are interested in the historical and theological roots of our climate crisis, I commend this little-noticed book to you.) In Bacon's horizon there is no restraint on human exploration or human exploitation. Thus, Bacon provided a ground for modern exploration that leads to *commoditization* of the earth and its vulnerable inhabitants, to *colonialization* that gave white

1. Wybrow, *Bible, Baconianism*, 18.

Europeans access to and legitimacy about confiscation of the resources of the world, and eventually to *industrialization* without restraint or regulation.

All of this is nicely summed up in the aphorism attributed to Bacon, "Knowledge is power." Bacon, of course, had in mind a certain kind of knowledge that was dependent upon a certain kind of reasoning that assured the advantage of white Europeans. Thus the modern world is constituted by a quest for unrestrained knowledge that has issued in insatiable technological scientific possibility. The outcome of course has been a mixed lot; great gains on the one hand for health and well-being, but on the other hand huge devastation of the earth by war, by confiscation, and by pollution among other things has been unleashed. We are able to see that Bacon's perspective of "knowledge as power" is intrinsically permeated with violence or at least potential violence. This Bacon could write in an appeal to the myth of Proteus:

> And thus far the fable reaches of Proteus, and his flock, at liberty and unrestrained. For the universe, with the common structures and fabrics of the creatures, is the face of matter, not under constraint, or . . . wrought upon and tortured by human means . . . And that method of binding, torturing, or detaining, will prove the most effectual and expeditious, which makes use of manacles, and fetters; that is, lays hold and works upon matter in the extremest degrees.[2]

Wybrow comments:

> Here then, is still another feature of Baconian science. It is not merely curious about secrets, not merely violent and rapacious in probing into those secrets, but subtly, craftily, calculatingly violent, employing the torture of experimental procedures. This torture, unlike simple domination, forces natural objects not only to gratify man (as the older arts sought to do), but to reveal their

2. Wybrow, *Bible, Baconianism*, 180, quoting Bacon, *Wisdom of the Ancients*.

inmost natures to him and hence to render themselves
open to all future forms of manipulation.[3]

The Bible of course, long before Bacon, maintained a critique
of such knowledge that yields autonomous, unrestrained power. In
the twin triads of Jeremiah "wisdom" is marked along with power
and wealth as seductions that contradict YHWH (Jer 9:23–24). In
this horizon "wisdom" clearly refers to the human capacity to pen-
etrate the mysteries of creation for the sake of control. This "wisdom" is judged negatively not out of obscurantism but because of
awe before the wonder of creation. That seductive triad of *wisdom,
wealth,* and *power* is juxtaposed by the prophet to the covenantal
triad of *justice, righteousness,* and *faithfulness.* By this simple ei-
ther/or (echoed by Paul in 1 Corinthians 1) Jeremiah mounts a
critique of the kind of power he observed in royal Jerusalem that
Bacon subsequently championed (see also 1 Kgs 4:29–34; and
Prov 25:2–3).

In a quite different idiom Israel's wisdom teachers averred
that true wisdom (unlike the Promethean wisdom of Jeremiah 9)
begins with reference to YHWH:

> The fear of the LORD is the beginning of wisdom;
> Fools despise wisdom and instruction. (Prov 1:7)

This is a very different "wisdom" that by reference to YHWH is
restrained and under covenantal discipline. Thus the capacity for
human knowledge is in the presence of YHWH that makes human
knowledge penultimate and challenged by the reality of YHWH
who cares for justice, righteousness, and faithfulness in the practice of knowledge. This thesis of Prov 1:7 is further exposited in the
poem of Job 28:1–28. After the poet considers the human capacity
for exploration of the earth and its resources, the poem is haunted
by the question:

> But where shall wisdom be found?
> And where is the place of understanding? . . .

3. Wybrow, *Bible, Baconianism,* 180.

> Where then does wisdom come from?
>   And where is the place of understanding?
>   (Job 28:12, 20)

The poem, in response to these questions, comes finally to reference YHWH the creator:

> Truly the fear of the Lord, that is wisdom;
>   and to depart from evil is understanding. (v. 28)

The second line of "depart from evil" indicates that genuine wisdom has a covenantal dimension to it, the very dimension that Bacon intended to exclude. Knowledge that is amoral is inimical to YHWH and is sure to be destructive. Thus, Bacon (and the future he has adumbrated) stand from the outset under the sharp critique of the covenantal tradition of Israel.

But then consider the Apostle Paul. When he wrote 1 Corinthians 13, he did not have in mind a romantic text to be used at all kinds of weddings for folk who knew nothing about and cared nothing about self-giving *agape*. Rather his pastoral concern is for the church in Corinth, seemingly his most conflicted congregation. It is easy to imagine the congregation in some dispute over various gifts . . . apostles, prophets, teachers, a capacity for leadership, tongues, and healing (see 12:27–31). Such various gifts were divisive in the church concerning who has the best or most important gifts. If we look at the inventory of gifts they variously concern different capacities that depend on specialized skills and knowledge.

Paul counters these conflicting claims with his accent on *agape* love in chapter 13. He asserts that specialized knowledge of any sort is not the best gift. He reassesses these claimed advantages in the community. He refuses the divisive claims of superior knowledge of any specialized sort, making all such knowledge distinctly penultimate (see Job 28). And then he dismisses them with his stunning triad:

> but do not have love . . . a noisy gong!
> but do not have love . . . I am nothing!
> but do not have love . . . I gain nothing!

None of these celebrated gifts matters at all if they are not marked by *agape*. Paul is impatient with and dismissive of gifts of knowledge in the church that are devoid of love. What a shock it must have been in the congregation to have their best claims discounted: *gong, nothing, nothing!* It turns out that these gifts amount to a "gong show" without significance or lasting importance.

So imagine Paul meeting Bacon. Bacon is full of knowledge. He does not doubt that knowledge can and will deliver control (colonialization, industrialization, commoditization) that will lead to a good life that can be embraced without restraint. And Paul counters:

— Don't count on *knowledge*;

— Don't count on *colonialization* that will prove toxic;

— Don't count on *commoditization* that will render all of life as a saleable good to the highest bidder;

— Don't count on *industrialization* that will let us master the universe but deeply trouble the environment.

All of that . . . knowledge, colonialization, commoditization, industrialization . . . *noisy gong, clanging cymbal, nothing!* Unless permeated with *agape*. Paul joins issue, early and late, with the Promethean life that is devoid of self-giving. Love is the greatest reality because God is love and has ordered creation for the performance of self-giving love. There is no way to circumvent this elemental reality, try as we will!

We are presently in a great contest between *Paul and Bacon*, between *love and knowledge*, between *neighbor and self-serving and self-seeking*.

It happens—I am not making this up!—that former President Trump is the point person for "knowledge," the generic term that subsumes colonialization, commoditization, and industrialization. After all,

— he knows more about the virus than the scientists.

He knows the most. And he assures us that his good judgment will make us safe and happy. He is not the whole team. He is only the point person. There many players on the team in our society. But he was the captain of the team, and it was all a noisy gong . . . a gong show!

And now as always, the church is an odd alternative community that gathers regularly to hear Paul and his ilk (and Moses before him!) yet again. We gather to remember that "the greatest of these is love." We gather to consider what we have learned from Moses that is reiterated by Paul:

> For the whole Torah is summed up in a single command-ment, "You shall love your neighbor as yourself." (Gal 5:14)

Love is kind, love is patient, love is long-suffering, love is durable. Love is, to be sure, vulnerable and fragile, but it is nonetheless the truth. It is the truth peculiarly entrusted to us. It is the truth that defies failed power, that instructs our best learning, and that pervades our greatest hopes.

We can see the drama of knowledge and love played out in our treasured narrative of Friday and Sunday. On Friday the efficient sure knowledge undergirding Rome prevailed. The empire with its powerful performance of legitimacy claimed ultimacy. But then on Sunday, something inscrutable happened that defied the empire. Now love—self-giving *agape love*—has its say. It is a drama played over and over. We are, all of us, so much excessively compelled by noisy gongs and clanging cymbals. But we know better. We know that self-giving love is the truth of God's world. That self-giving love is the clue to peace, justice, prosperity, and well-being. While the world heeds the noise of the gong, we know better; for that reason we may live (and invest and organize and advocate) differently!

BIBLIOGRAPHY

Bacon, Francis. *The Wisdom of the Ancients.* 1609. Reprint, in *The Works of Francis Bacon,* 701–64. Cambridge: Cambridge University Press, 2011.

Baptist, Edward E. *The Half Has Never Been Told: Slavery and the Story of American Capitalism.* New York: Basic Books, 2016.

Barth, Karl. *Church Dogmatics.* Vol. 4, *The Doctrine of Reconciliation, Part 1.* Edited by G. W. Bromiley and T. F. Torrance. Translated by G. W. Bromiley. Edinburgh: T. & T. Clark, 1956.

Boer, Roland. *The Sacred Economy in Ancient Israel.* Library of Ancient Israel. Louisville: Westminster John Knox, 2015.

Bradley, James. *The Imperial Cruise: A Secret History of Empire and War.* New York: Little, Brown, 2009.

Brueggemann, Walter. *1 & 2 Kings.* Smyth & Helwys Bible Commentary. Macon, GA: Smyth & Helwys, 2000.

———. "The Proclamation of the Resurrection in the Old Testa-ment." In *Truth-Telling as Subversive Obedience,* edited by K. C. Hanson, 41–52. Eugene, OR: Cascade Books, 2011.

———. "Truth-Telling as Subversive Obedience." In *Truth-Telling as Subversive Obedience,* edited by K. C. Hanson, 68–80. Eugene, OR: Cascade Books, 2011.

Compton, John. *The End of Empathy: Why White Protestants Stopped Loving Their Neighbors.* New York: Oxford University Press, 2020.

Davis, David Brion. *The Problem of Slavery in the Age of Emancipation, 1770–1823.* Power and Morality Collection at Harvard Business School. Ithaca, NY: Cornell University Press, 1975.

Douthat, Ross. "It's Trump's Revolution." *New York Times,* June 13, 2020. https://www.nytimes.com/2020/06/13/opinion/sunday/trump-presidency.html.

Fishbane, Michael. *Sacred Attunement: A Jewish Theology.* Chicago: University of Chicago Press, 2008.

Glory to God: The Presbyterian Hymnal. Louisville: Westminster John Knox, 2013.

Graeber, David. *Debt: The First 5000 Years.* Brooklyn: Melville House, 2010.

———. *The Utopia of Rules: On Technology, Stupidity, and the Secret Joys of Bureaucracy*. Brooklyn: Melville House, 2015.

Johnson, Walter. *The Broken Heart of America: St. Louis and the Violent History of the United States*. New York: Basic Books, 2020.

King, Martin Luther, Jr. "Remaining Awake through a Great Revolution." Speech at the National Cathedral, Washington, DC, March 31, 1968. **Audio**: https://www.youtube.com/watch?v=SLsXZXJAURk. **Transcript**: https://www.caribbeannationalweekly.com/caribbean-breaking-news-featured/mlk-jr-remaining-awake-revolution/.

Lane, Nathan C. *The Compassionate but Punishing God: A Canonical Analysis of Exodus 34:6–7*. Eugene, OR: Pickwick, 2010.

Levenson, Jon D. *The Death and Resurrection of the Beloved Son: The Transformation of Child Sacrifice in Judaism and Christianity*. New Haven: Yale University Press, 1993.

———. *Resurrection and the Restoration of Israel: The Ultimate Victory of the God of Life*. New Haven: Yale University Press, 2006.

Madigan, Kevin J., and Jon D. Levenson. *Resurrection: The Power of God for Christians and Jews*. New Haven: Yale University Press, 2008.

Mather, Cotton. *Magnalia Christi Americana; or, The Ecclesiastical History of New-England, from Its First Planting in the Year 1620 unto the Year of Our Lord, 1698*. London: Parkhurst, 1702.

McMahon, Paul. *Feeding Frenzy: Land Grabs, Price Spikes, and the World Food Crisis*. Berkeley: Greystone, 2014.

Morgan, Dan. *Merchants of Grain: The Power and Profits of the Five Grain Companies at the Center of the World's Food Supply*. New York: Viking, 1979.

Nelson, Janet L. *King and Emperor: A New Life of Charlemagne*. London: Allen Lane, 2019.

Pearce, Fred. *The Land Grabbers: The New Fight over Who Owns the Earth*. Boston: Beacon, 2012.

Premnath, D. N. *Eighth Century Prophets: A Social Analysis*. St. Louis: Chalice, 2003.

Said, Edward. "Permission to Narrate." *London Review of Books*, 1984. Reprinted in *The Selected Works of Edward Said, 1966–2006*, edited by Moustafa Bayoumi and Andrew Rubin, 245–68. New York: Vintage, 2019.

Schafer, Roy. *Retelling a Life: Narration and Dialogue in Psychoanalysis*. New York: Basic Books, 1992.

Scott, James C. *Against the Grain: A Deep History of the Earliest States*. Yale Agrarian Studies. New Haven: Yale University Press, 2017.

Shah, Sonia. *The Next Great Migration: The Beauty and Terror of Life on the Move*. New York: Bloomsbury, 2020.

Sharp, Carolyn. *Joshua*. Smyth & Helwys Bible Commentary. Macon, GA: Smyth & Helwys, 2019.

Tennyson, Alfred Lord. "In Memoriam A.H.H." (1833). Reprinted in Paul Turner, *Tennyson*. Routledge Author Guides. London: Routledge & Kegan Paul, 1976.

Trible, Phyllis. *God and the Rhetoric of Sexuality.* Overtures to Biblical Theology. Philadelphia: Fortress, 1978.

The United Methodist Hymnal: Book of United Methodist Worship. Nashville: United Methodist Publishing, 1989.

Wallace, George. Inauguration speech. January 14, 1963. https://www.blackpast.org/african-american-history/speeches-african-american-history/1963-george-wallace-segregation-now-segregation-forever/.

Wallis, Jim. *America's Original Sin: Racism, White Privilege, and the Bridge to a New America.* Grand Rapids: Brazos, 2016.

———. "The Virus of White Supremacy." *Sojourner,* August 2020. https://sojo.net/magazine/august-2020/virus-white-supremacy.

Weegmann, Martin. *Permission to Narrate: Explorations in Group Analysis, Psychoanalysis, Culture.* London: Routledge, 2016.

Westover, Tara. *Educated: A Memoir.* New York: Random House, 2018.

Whelan, Matthew Philipp. *Blood in the Fields: Óscar Romero, Catholic Social Teaching, and Land Reform.* Washington, DC: Catholic University of America Press, 2020.

Wybrow, Cameron. *The Bible, Baconianism, and Mastery over Nature: The Old Testament and Its Modern Misreading.* American University Studies, Series 7, Theology and Religion 112. New York: Lang, 1991.

Yoder, John C. *Power and Politics in the Book of Judges: Men and Women of Valor.* Minneapolis: Fortress, 2015.

SCRIPTURE INDEX

NAME INDEX

Schafer, Roy, 13
Scott, James C., 85, 89–90
Seeger, Pete, 119
Shah, Sonia, 57
Shakespeare, William, 104
Sharp, Carolyn, 84–85
Styron, William, 47

Taylor, Adam, 61
Tennyson, Alfred Lord, 3
Trible, Phyllis, 99–100

Trump, Donald J., 1, 65–66, 111,
    118–19, 125
Turner, Paul, 3

Wallace, George, 52
Wallis, Jim, 25, 57–61
Weegmann, Martin, 13, 18
Welch, Joseph, 37
Westover, Tara, 108–9
Whelan, Matthew Philipp, 75–77
Wybrow, Cameron, 121–23

Yoder, John C., 28

Printed in Great Britain
by Amazon

86918590R00089